ALB[A]

Corfu

GREECE

The Ionian Islands

Lefkas

Ithaki

Kefalonia

MEDITERRANEAN SEA

N

W — E

S

0   40miles

0   60Km

Zakynthos

MEDITERRANEAN SUNSEEKERS
CORFU

Brian & Eileen Anderson

MPC

Contents

KEY TO SYMBOLS USED IN TEXT MARGIN AND ON MAPS

Recommended walks

Aquatic interest

Castle/Fortification

Other place of interest

Beach

Water sports

Garden

Church/Ecclesiastical site

Building of interest

Archaeological site

Museum/Art Gallery

Beautiful view/Scenery, Natural phenomenon

Birdlife

Airport

Nature Reserve/Animal interest

Golf

interesting Railway

Caves

Parkland

Mountain/Notch

Tourist information

KEY TO MAPS

———————— Main Routes (Surfaced)

———————— Secondary Routes (Surfaced)

------------ Track

Town

Village

River/Lake

HOW TO USE THIS GUIDE

Enjoying as much sun and fun on a vacation is everyone's dream. *Mediterranean Sunseekers: Corfu* will help to make this dream come true. Your guide has been designed in easy to use sections.

'The Introduction is packed with detailed information on the island, its history, geography, people, culture, food and much more. 'Out and About Corfu' is a comprehensive itinerary covering the island with a series of useful and practical motoring or walking tours. Many places are off the beaten track and not on the usual tourist circuit. 'Facts for Visitors' arranged in alphabetical order for easy reference, lists practical information and useful advice to help you plan your vacation before you go and while you are there.

Distinctive margin symbols in the text and on maps, plus places to visit highlighted in bold enable the reader to find the most interesting places with ease.

Introduction

There are no regular paths for falling in love nor regular reasons, so explaining why so many visitors regularly fall in love with Corfu could take some time. Sketching in the main chemistry is easy enough. Alluring landscapes hide around every corner and high mountains add drama to the north. Three million olive trees and a rage of wild flowers give a verdancy which is as unexpected as it is pleasing and a scalloped coastline hides, like the oyster hides pearls, coves of great natural beauty. On top of all this the people are kind and friendly and the island is continually drenched in sunshine throughout summer. It may be that some visitors are thrilled to see old folk still riding donkeys out in the countryside or old ladies wearing Corfiot costume. Or is it simply scents of orange, lemon and thyme wafting on the summer breezes? Whatever the lure, it has never failed over the centuries and the power is still as strong. The island probably has more lovers than Aphrodite.

Corfu boasts that it was the first island in Greece to welcome tourism and over the years it has been highly successful in attracting visitors in great numbers. It might be easy to conclude that the island has matured and that its resorts have reached a state of over-development. Surprisingly perhaps, this is just not the case. It is true that many resorts have developed but high rise buildings have generally been eschewed in favour of smaller hotels and apartments. It is equally true that other resorts have been less inclined to develop at all with the pleasing result that Corfu is an island which can offer a resort for virtually every taste. It can cater for visitors who want to party the night away and bask in the sun all day to those who prefer a quiet away-from-it-all holiday with perhaps some country walking or gentle sight seeing during the day. The whole spectrum of choice is there and to help with the decision making a resort guide is included below which offers a thumbnail sketch of the main places.

GREEK NATIONAL TOURIST OFFICE

Leaflets on Corfu and general information is available from the Greek National Tourist Office, as follows:

UK and Ireland, 4 Conduit Street, London W1R 0DJ ☎ 0171 734 599

USA, 645 Fifth Avenue, Olympic Tower (5th Floor), New York NY10022 ☎ 421 57777;

168 North Michigan Avenue, Chicago, Illinois 60601 ☎ 728 1084

611 West 6th Street, Suite 2198 Los Angeles, California 90017 ☎ 626 696

Australia & New Zealand, 51-57 Pitt Street, Sydney, NSW 2000 ☎ 241 1663

Preceding page: Kalami, where tavernas front on to the shingle beach

A Touch of Geography

Corfu is one of Greece's most westerly islands and lies in the Ionian sea very close to the part of the Greek mainland which borders Albania. It is the second largest, and most populous (108,000 in 1991) of the seven Ionian islands and somewhat oddly shaped, rather like a comma seen through a mirror. At its widest point in the north, it stretches to almost 20 miles (32km) while its length is double that at 40 miles (64km). Neighbouring islands to the south include Paxos and Antipaxos.

Crossing the island to the north is a range of rugged hills which rise to a peak with Pandokrator (3,000ft/914km). There is another range of high ground hugging the west coast, giving great character to the resorts on that side of the island, and culminating in the islands second highest peak, Ag. Deka (1890ft/576m). In the middle of the island sits the fertile Ropa Plain and there is more level ground to the south of the island. Wetlands too exist in the south, in the catchment area of the Messongi River and around Lake Korission.

When To Go

Easter time in April is about the earliest that can be considered. Even at this time there is a risk that the weather will be cold and showery but, if the sun is shining, the island is at its most beautiful. At this time the sea is still cold but the sun is easily hot enough to burn and sunbathers still need to take care. Spring is a delightful season for colour when the trees are achingly green and the wild flowers at their very best. Fortunately, the spring flowers extend into May and May is generally more reliable for weather. Daytime temperatures start to rise but the evenings are still cool. It is not always warm enough to dine outside in the evening in the early part of the month but night-time temperatures too are on the rise and it soon becomes possible, well before the month is out. The island has plenty of visitors in these early months but not enough to make it busy with the result that, although bars and tavernas are usually in full swing, some of the water sports and perhaps discos have not yet opened.

Things warm up in June in every sense. The days and nights get hotter and the island tourist machine moves into top gear. Nowhere is too crowded and independent visitors can still expect to find accommodation without too much trouble. All that changes in July, with the Greeks and Italians moving into their holiday season, and the island suddenly becomes very crowded. July and August are the hottest months of the year and the least comfortable on the island. Beaches are full and the facilities often at full stretch.

Even the locals welcome September when the crowds have departed and some of the intense heat leaves the sun. Many regard September as the best month of the summer with

Sunseeker
Hot Spots

Places not to be missed on Corfu:

Above: Kassiopi. Beautiful port, good waterside atmosphere
Facing page, above: Corfu Town. Venetian atmosphere, old narrow streets, forts and museums
Facing page, below: Paleokastritsa. Beauty spot, nice beaches, monastery and walks
Below: Kanoni. For Mouse Island, the most photographed spot on Corfu

the sea still warm and the sun still pouring incessantly from the sky although the autumn rains may well start before the month is out. October is cooler with more cloudy and rainy days but still with fine, sunny periods.

CLIMATE

Corfu enjoys a fairly typical Mediterranean climate which in simple terms means mild, wet winters and hot dry summers. As always, there are variations within any climatic type and Corfu varies fairly considerably from the norm. Overall, Corfu has a high annual rainfall, somewhere in the region of 45in (115cm), which is higher than most other Greek islands and almost three times more than Crete. Fortunately for holiday-makers, most of this rain falls in the winter months, between October and March. Summers are not entirely without rain but usually in the form of thunderstorms which may be heavy but short lived. All this translates to good news for summer visitors, the heavy winter rainfall ensures the island stays luxuriously green throughout the whole year and that taps do not run dry or showers dry up at the height of the tourist season.

January and February are the coldest months and even then average maximum daytime temperatures of around 14°C (67°F) are enjoyed. Frost is rare and snow seen only on the distant hills in Albania. Spring comes early, judging by the flowers, as early as February but March and April are the main spring months. Sometimes the increase in temperatures from spring to summer is steady but just occasionally it is very rapid and the summer heat starts early.

Summer is long and hot with May, June, averaging daily more than 10 and 11 hours of sunshine respectively while July and August enjoy around 12 and 13.

Autumn rains arrive fairly early in Corfu compared to other Greek islands, usually sometime in September although temperatures stay fairly high. October starts the six really wet months of winter but even then more than 6 hours of sunshine are still expected every day.

Compared with the Aegean islands which suffer steady winds throughout the summer, Corfu is relatively calm although the maestro blowing from the north-west can rise in the afternoon only to settle again in the evenings. The worst of the winds is the siroccos blowing up from North Africa which brings a heavy haze and hot, sticky conditions, although the humidity is high on the island all summer. It is unlikely that any Corfiot would seriously complain about the climate, it produces ideal growing conditions which has in the past brought the island considerable prosperity and its fine summers are bringing a new prosperity through tourism.

Resort Guide

Holiday brochures try to make each and every resort sound attractive without always revealing too much about its character. This guide offers a quick outline of the main resorts on the island to help in making the most suitable choice. A more detailed description of the resorts may be found by consulting the Touring and Exploring section and those marked with an asterisk are also featured in the Good Beach Guide also included in this section. Water sport facilities are indicated by symbols. One ⚓ indicates very limited facilities, perhaps just pedaloes or simply boats for hire, while the maximum three indicates the whole gamut from paragliding, jet skis, banana rides down to the less energetic pursuits but remember, full facilities are not always available early and late in the season.

Corfu Town: it has a lot in its favour, interesting streets to wander, good eating, night-life, the hub of the bus network but it is not normally regarded as a resort although there are some large hotels. Sun bathing space down by the old fort and a pay beach at the far end of Garitsa Bay.

East coast, south of Corfu Town:

Kanoni: just to the south of Corfu town, this peninsula is the resort area for the town. Very close to the busy airport so expect noise. Most of the hotels fit nicely into the wooded slopes, little in the way of beaches but handy for Mouse Island.

Perama: swallowed up by the busy main road which carries traffic down to the south of the island.

Benitses: lively resort with good night life but hard to explain why. It has a poor, narrow shingle beach backed by a busy main road. Old village spreads inland into the mountains and adds a little character which is otherwise missing. ⚓⚓

Mora'i'tika*: an emerging resort with a nice beach of sand/shingle. The main shops along the main road inland from beach. Offers a rare mixture of quiet and lively, good for families. ⚓⚓

Messongi: quiet resort at the mouth of a river of the same name. Tiny, attractive centre, narrow sand/shingle beach, dominated by big hotels but always seems more dead than alive. Low on character.

Kavos*: this is where the young party the night away and recover on the beach next day. The whole resort throbs incessantly to the beat of music both day and night. Lovely beach, plenty of water sports but best left to the young. ⚓⚓⚓

Following page: The narrow shingle beach at Ipsos

Above: Achilleion Palace. Nineteenth-century romantic palace and gardens

Below: The Palace of St Michael and St John

East coast, north of Corfu town:

Kondokali: hard to describe as a resort. It lies at the neck of a small peninsula looking towards Gouvia bay, just off the main road and seems little more than a line of shops dedicated to tourism. Might be possible to find a spot by the water but the only beach is by the large hotel and that man-made.

Gouvia: attractively set in arcing bay but beach largely shingle. No centre as such but the heart of the resort lies along the road inland from the beach. Plenty of everything from tourists shops to bars in this lively resort.

Dassia: a long narrow sand/shingle beach punctuated here and there with wooden platforms for water sports or sun bathing. Café bars and tavernas open onto beach but main road with all the major facilities about 500yd inland. A popular, lively resort which gets crowded in summer.

Ipsos (and Pyrgi): hard to know how it came to be a resort. A long, narrow shingle beach running alongside the noisy main road. This place can hardly be called attractive but the younger set seem to like it for its bars and night-life. Pyrgi shares the northern end of the same bay.

Barbati*: a tiny resort perched at the foot of Mount Pandokrator. Accommodation along the road but below lies a picturesque beach, long sweep of white pebbles. A quiet but attractive resort.

Nissaki: another small but very picturesque resort. Accommodation scattered on hillside, small beach, very scenic and a great place to get away from it all.

North coast, from east to west:

Kassiopi: this has recently grown into a thriving resort built around a picturesque harbour and old village. Plenty of character but the beaches are small and disappointing, not so good for children. Moderately lively, harbour is busy during the day with trippers arriving by coach and boat and there are bars and discotheques enough for those seeking some night-life.

Acharavi: lies adjacent to Ag Stefanos (not to be confused with the one on the west coast) and is almost indistinguishable. One of the newly developing resorts which is in effect an extension of Roda and shares the same bay. Plenty of modern accommodation but lacks character.

Roda*: good family resort with long sandy beach. A fairly modern, straggling town which is interesting rather than attractive, although older part adds some character. It has a full range of facilities with sufficient bars and disco for those seeking some night-life.

Sidari*: modern, attractive resort, good for families. Two large sandy bays with good access, plenty of facilities and lively enough.

West coast from north to south:

Ag. Stefanos: small but growing resort set in attractive crescent shaped, sandy bay. Much of the development is scattered taking place away from beach, has potential but does not really hang together just yet. Expect it to be quiet. ⚓ ⚓

Ag. Georgiou (north)*: although fairly isolated it is an attractive, self sufficient resort with narrow but good sandy beach. Plenty of facilities, good atmosphere and on the quiet side.

Paleokastritsa*: an area of great natural beauty which has developed into an ungainly resort without any real identity. Much of the accommodation straggles thinly for almost 2 miles up the approach road. Good beaches but crowded with day trippers. ⚓ ⚓ ⚓

Liapades: the village itself is large and full of character but lies inland and uphill from the beach. Much of the accommodation lies close to the small, sandy/shingle Elli beach with another small beach, the mainly shingle Rovinia beach, just a short walk away. Interesting, small in terms of resort accommodation and quiet. ⚓

Ermones: attractive but tiny resort. Steep descent to small sand and shingle beach which is supported by taverna and bar facilities at beach level.

Glifada*: picturesque resort reached after a long winding descent. Good beach with accommodation, hotel, apartments and studios, as well as other facilities down at beach level. Good family resort and fairly quiet. ⚓ ⚓

Pelekas*: starting to develop as a resort. Pelekas, an old village full of character, is wrapped around the mountainside in a scenic area of the island while the long, sandy beach is quite a way down below. Some accommodation lies in the village and some down by the beach. ⚓

Ag. Gordis*: small resort in attractive location. Its best feature is a long sandy beach ringed by wooded hills and cliffs. Good facilities, some night-life but generally quiet.

Ag. Georgios (south)*: modern resort still developing but with no real centre. Fine sandy beach with plenty of facilities, good for families but isolated. ⚓ ⚓

GETTING THERE

The easiest way is by charter flight directly from a regional airport in the U.K. and there are many tour operators offering packaged holi-

Mainland Hopping

Corfu makes a very convenient base for a two centre holiday but it needs a little planning beforehand. With a hire car it is very easy to escape over to Igoumenitsa on the mainland which instantly opens up a whole new range of possibilities. Here are a few suggestions;

IOANNINA AND METEORA Lakeside Ioannina is about 2 hours drive from Igoumenitsa and will easily fill a couple of days. After that head over the Katara pass to look at the mountain village of Metsovo at 1,160m (3,804ft) and on to Meteora to see the spectacular monasteries perched on rock columns.

IOANNINA AND ZAGORIA Little known Zagoria is an area of great natural beauty full of delightful hill villages and it provides great opportunities for serious walkers, like the incredible Vikos Gorge which is even more striking than its famous counterpart in Crete, the Samaria Gorge.

LEFKAS It is an easy drive down the mainland and onto the island of Lefkas which is not strictly an island since it is joined to the mainland by a causeway.

Details of all these locations can be found in Visitor's Guide to Greece (Moorland Publishing Co. Ltd).

KEFALONIA This also can be reached within the day by driving on to Lefkas and ferrying either from Nidri or Vasiliki to Fiskardo on Kefalonia. For further details of Kefalonia see the Sunseekers guide for this island.

Above: Kalami, north of Ipsos

Below: Georgios, the south beach

days to the island. Travel agents generally only deal with a limited number of tour operators and if they are unable to offer the required destination, they will, on request, find out from a directory which operators do serve the particular resort. It may be necessary to change to a travel agent who deals with the company to book a holiday.

For those planning to stay longer than the usual two or three weeks, it may be necessary to travel on scheduled flights from London to Athens then from Athens to Corfu. There are many carriers offering flights to Athens but only Olympic Airways flying between Athens and Corfu. This may change shortly since there are now a number of new carriers in Greece opening up flights to the islands. Usually the journey from the UK can be accomplished in one day without the need for an overnight stop in Athens.

The scheduled route into Athens with an onward flight to Corfu is the only option from North America, although many Americans find it more economical to fly into London and join a packaged holiday from there . Flights from America to Athens may not connect up conveniently with the limited Corfu flights to Corfu. If an overnight stop is required there is a hotel reservations desk at the airport. Hotels near the airport tend to be noisy so, for a quieter night, it is better to choose a city centre hotel.

PASSPORTS AND JABS

There are no visa requirements for EU citizens or other English speaking nationals (USA, Australia, Canada, New Zealand) for visits of up to 3 months. All that is required is a valid passport.

Certain inoculations are advisable for all travellers (hepatitis A, tetanus, typhoid and TB) but none are mandatory for Greece.

ESSENTIAL THINGS TO PACK

Since Greece is a full member of the EU, it is very likely that, should you forget your favourite brand of toothpaste, you will be able to buy it in the shops there. All leading brands of food and products are freely available, give or take some national peculiarities. Brands of tea and breakfast cereal fall into this category, however, a limited range of breakfast cereals can be bought in most tourist regions. With tea it is a little easier, if you have a favourite brand of tea or tea bags then it is easy to find room for some in your luggage.

There are a few other items which are worth considering if only to save time shopping when you are there.

An electric mosquito repeller and tablets — these are readily available in Greece but small 'travel' types are freely available in UK shops which are a convenient size for packing and will last for years. Make sure you buy one with a continental 2 pin plug. Insect repellent — if you prefer a particular brand, buy it at home. Anthisan cream for insect bites. Folding umbrella, particularly if you are visiting Corfu outside the main season. Rain showers tend to be short and, with the rain falling straight down, an umbrella gives good protection, better than a waterproof which can quickly make you hot and sweaty. A small rucksack is useful too for general use when heading for the beach or off on a shopping trip.

Only in early season is it necessary to take a heavy jumper but it is always useful to take some thinner layers of clothing which you can wear together. Sometimes it is cool in the evening or you may feel cool after the heat of the sun. If you intend to do any serious walking make sure you have suitable footwear.

Most basic medical requirements, plasters, bandages, headache pills can be bought in chemist shops on Corfu. More than that, many drugs normally available in Britain only on prescription can be bought over the counter on demand and at reasonable prices.

Note: that codeine and drugs containing codeine are strictly banned in Greece so be sure to exclude these from your luggage.

FOOD AND DRINK

Watching the Greeks eat is a pleasure in itself. Seldom do they order individually, instead they order a vast number of communal dishes which fill the table to overflowing. They are far less concerned about cold food and many dishes which arrive hot are cold before they are eaten. Some tourists find it a bit disconcerting when their meals are actually served on the cool side but, in most areas, the message that tourists generally like their food hot has registered.

Although the Greek cuisine is quite extensive, tavernas tend only to have a limited menu. Lunch time, between 2 and 3pm after work finishes, is the only meal of the day for which the chef will prepare a range of cooked dishes. For the evening trade, and the Greeks are notoriously late eaters, the menu offers whatever is left over from lunch, which has often been kept warm for hours, and a range of grills which are cooked to order. Charcoal is generally used for grilling and it is not unusual to see large charcoal grills by the doorway or outside in summer. Although the tavernas are the traditional eating places, Corfu town has a selection of restaurants which provide a better standard of décor in particular and offer a more international cuisine.

Tavernas are obliged to have a menu but many still don't. Instead diners will be shown a glass show case exhibiting the range of dishes available or, and this is still very common in the villages, they will be led into the kitchen to see exactly what is cooking. If difficulties are experienced in the final choice then spoons may appear for a tasting session. In an effort to improve stand-

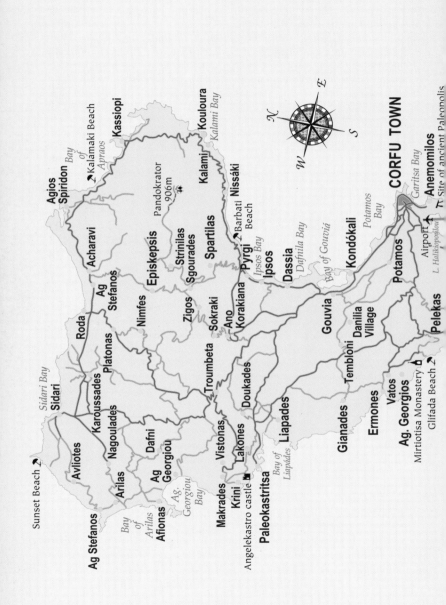

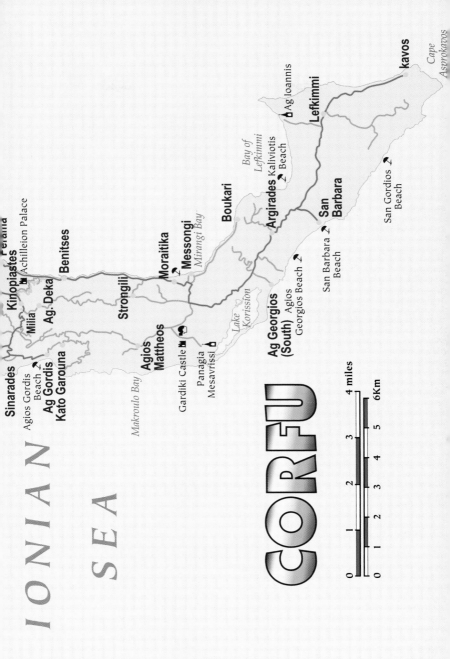

ards, there has been a recent government decree instructing that all tables should have a cloth table cloth. Previously it was usual just to have a plain piece of polythene which was changed for each new client. It served a double purpose because at the end of the meal all scraps from the plates would be tipped into it and the whole lot bundled up and removed. Now the situation has changed. Tables are fitted with a decorative table cloth but this is securely protected by a polythene sheet covered by paper square and only the latter is laid fresh each time. Should there be a menu on the table then it will probably be in Greek and English but it will only show a partial correspondence with the dishes on offer so it still pays to ask. It is unusual to find the table laid, apart from the oil and vinegar flasks, paper napkins and the inevitable toothpicks, but the cutlery arrives with bread after an order is placed.

There is no special form in a taverna and no conventions to follow. The Greeks often go in for a plate of chips and a beer and make it last half the night. For diners though, it is usual to begin with one or a selection of the starters or mezedes on offer. These include tzatsiki (a yoghurt, cucumber and garlic dip), taramasalata (fish roe mixed with potato, oil and vinegar, the pinker the better), melitzano salata (an aubergine dip with tomato and garlic) and humus, another dip this time from chick-peas. Fresh vegetables are rarely available but two vegetables which turn up as mezedes are gigantes (butter beans cooked in tomato and oil) and peas (arakas). Saganaki, fried cheese, is another interesting starter. The waiter will raise an eyebrow if mezedes are ordered separately by each individual, even tourists are expected to order a selection and share in Greek style. Salads may be preferred as starters or as part of the starters and the most popular is the village salad or horiatiki salata which should include lettuce, or cabbage, but less so now, tomato, onion, cucumber, feta cheese and olives. A few years ago, a salad like this constituted a meal in itself and many tourists were perfectly happy to make a lunch from it. Unfortunately, this made the taverna owner less than happy, consequently the price has risen considerably and they are not always the generous portions they were. Tomatoes, cucumber, feta cheese and lettuce (maruli) are all offered as separate dishes. Ready cooked dishes may include the familiar moussaka, a mince dish with aubergines, potato and bechamel sauce, veal in tomato (kokanista), stifado (veal stew with onions) or giovetsi (oven cooked lamb served with pasta). Chicken cooked on the spit is popular and inexpensive but favoured amongst the grills is souvlaki, veal or pork on a skewer. Chops, pork, lamb or veal, are ever present on the evening menus as are keftedes (spicy meat balls) and biftekia (mince burgers). One of Corfu's specialities is a dish called sofrito which is veal cooked in wine with herbs, garlic and vinegar and served with a thick sauce.

Fish is sometimes on offer but for a selection it is better to find a fish taverna, psaria taverna. Fish is becoming increasingly expensive and prices on the menu are often expressed per kilogram which makes them look sky high. In practice, a fish is weighed off and the charge is for that weight. A typical portion is around 400grm. Lobster (astakos) and red mullet (barbounia) are usually top of the menu and are expensive as are shrimps (garides). Octopus, grilled or cooked in wine is less expensive as is squid (kalamari). At the cheap end is the small whitebait (marides) which is eaten in its entirety, head and all. This dish is often available as a starter in a fish restaurant. Deserts are very limited, usually fruit, but the popularity of yoghurt and honey amongst the tourists is now recognised. If you have tucked into your meal with obvious enjoyment, the proprietor may produce a plate of fruit, peeled and presented with his compliments.

Some Greeks prefer to drink ouzo with meals and this is served in small bottles and usually taken with water. Others choose retsina, a re-sinated wine, which is an acquired taste and the popular commercial brand is Kourtaki although Mel-amatina is equally good and slightly less resinated. Most wine lists contain some of the country's acknowledged good wines like Boutari Naoussa and Lac des Roches as well as some medium priced popular ones like Kambas, Rotonda and Domestica. Corfu grows plenty of vines but the island has no major wine factory so everybody makes their own and the local wine is much cheaper and usually good. Ask for *krasi dopio* (local wine) or *spitiko krasi* (house wine) which is usually served in a carafe or metal jug.

THE PEOPLE

In spite of the island's turbulent history and the parade of masters over the centuries, the people of Corfu have retained their own brand of Greekness. This Greekness, tempered by western influences, from the Venetians, the French and the British, over the centuries, is a little different from that observed in the more easterly parts but the language and the church provided a continuity which has kept the people in touch with their own identity. Their conviviality and hospitality to strangers wins the island many friends. Sadly, these qualities are subdued by the pressure of work in the height of the tourist season but never squashed. Away from all the bustle, it takes only a cheerful greeting, sometimes only a smile, to be on the receiving end of their hospitality. It may take the form of an orange pulled from a bag or a handful of freshly grown broad beans but whatever it is, it is considered bad manners to refuse. Language barriers do not exist for the Greeks and mostly they will chatter away in

Fast Food Greek Style

The Greeks are great nibblers, particularly in the mornings, so there is no shortage of fast-food.

'Pies' with various fillings, usually made with filo pastry and looking like a Cornish pasty:

TIROPITTA — cheese. This is the most universally popular and found everywhere.

SPANAKOPITTA — spinach only or with cheese and eggs.

KREATOPITTA — minced meat.

PIZZA — usually take-away small ones or sometimes sold as pieces.

and for the sweet tooth:

MILOPITTA — apple.

BOUGATZA — vanilla custard.

SOUVLAKI — small pieces of meat on a wooden skewer served with a lump of bread or with pitta.

DONER ME PITTA — slices of meat from the 'gyros' (meat cooked on a vertical spit) placed in a pitta parcel with a little yoghurt, tomato and onion.

TOST — usually a slice of ham and cheese toasted between bread.

Freshly pressed orange juice is widely available.

Above: Local shops are fun to explore if you are self-catering

Below: Corn drying on a pavement at Lefkimmi

their native tongue in the full expectancy that you will understand some or part of whatever they are saying. Body language and gesticulations play a full part too. The head is frequently used this way. Assent is signified by a slight nod to the side and no is indicted by a slight toss of the head upward often accompanied by a slight 'tchh' sound. If words fail, an invitation to come or to follow is mostly by a downward pawing movement of the hand. If this is an invitation into the home, the first offering will be some sweet preserves served with a glass of water. To refuse this is to refuse their hospitality but it is not essential to eat all of it. No matter how poor the hosts, any suggestion of payment will cause deep offence but a small present for a child would be acceptable. The penetration of polite conversation often takes visitors by surprise. After the usual health enquiries, which are taken seriously by the Greeks, the conversation quickly moves into questions about the family, how many sons, daughters and their ages. Unreserved admiration is expressed for parents of large families especially with many sons. From this point enquiries continue about work and will invariably contain a question which throws unprepared visitors almost into a state of shock; 'How much do you earn?' In Greek society it would be considered impolite not to ask.

The family unit is strong and still the basis of Greek society, although there are signs that the bonds are starting to weaken under western influences. It is sons who receive the adulation and are totally spoilt by their parents. This does not mean that daughters are not welcomed, as in some societies, and the ideal family is regarded as one son and one daughter. It is remarkable just how many Greek families comprise just two children. In reality they have been using abortion as a means of birth control for a long time. Parental influence is still strong when the time is right for their children to marry. Arranged marriages have not entirely disappeared but they are no longer the norm but parents still have a dominant role in satisfying the demands of society and tradition. It is the duty of the son to stand by his parents to ensure that suitable matches are made for all his sisters before he can contemplate marriage. Although a dowry is no longer a legal requirement, and this repeal was only in recent times, it is still perpetuated. A girl goes into marriage often with the gift of a furnished house or apartment from her parents. It remains the girls property and her security. In the same way gifts of gold to the bride, also to provide for her security, are not unusual. At least the newly wedded couple start life without the burden of debt and are able to build and plan a future for their own children. The family unit extends into business too. The Greek preference is for self employment, failing that a secure job with the state, and most of the small businesses employ only family which are eventually passed down via sons and daughters.

It is a male dominated society in which it is demeaning for a man to indulge in women's tasks. This distinct role division is ingrained into society and a woman would lose face if her man was seen sweeping floors or washing dishes. Attitudes are slowly changing amongst the younger generation. The segregation of the sexes too is inbuilt into society. When family or friends enjoy a meal in a taverna, which can be quite a boisterous affair, there is usually a polarisation where the men cluster to one end of the table and the women to the other. Only men have the freedom to go out alone and it is not uncommon to see them dining out in groups but the young mostly head for the bars and congregate there in large numbers. Again signs of change are evident even in this area and young women are becoming part of the social scene. The role of women in the broader society has been recognised in legislation. They acquired the vote only in 1952 and the first woman Deputy was elected to Parliament the following year. Sexual discrimination in career opportunities and in the place of work has been outlawed. Many practical steps have been taken to assist the integration of women as equals in society. Low cost nurseries providing child places have been provided to free women to work and they have acquired rights of ownership after marriage and an equal share of communal property on divorce. Women now hold important posts in all branches of the Civil Service and in commerce but, in spite of all their progress, equality is only accepted in the big cities. Throughout rural Greece it remains contrary to the culture and fundamental change will only be fully accepted very slowly. For women travelling alone in Greece there are no exceptional problems. The incidence of violent crime, including rape, is much lower than in other western societies. But it is not unknown and the same wariness of the possible situations should be observed. Greek men firmly believe that they are irresistible to all women so their attentions can be expected. Corfu has been involved in tourism for a long time, is very cosmopolitan and women alone in bars or tavernas is totally accepted.

ARTS AND CULTURE

One legacy of the Venetian rule is music and Corfu town has a number of town bands who perform on ceremonial occasions or at festivals in their colourful, bright red uniforms. From June onwards there are regular concerts on the bandstand on the Esplanade (details from the tourist office). Some of the villages have bands and the town also has a Philharmonic Orchestra and a choir.

Greek dancing is popular on the island and local dancers often perform in restaurants and tavernas throughout the season. Many of the

Following page: The local people add interest as you travel around

Above: End of the day in Doukades

Below: Laden donkeys can be a hazard to motorists in rural areas. Bear this in mind if you are hiring a car

dances are local to Corfu or the Epirus region but programmes usually include the more popular dances performed throughout the country.

Two places to see organised displays of Greek dancing are at Danilia Village (see page 84) where it is performed every night as part of a typical Greek evening and the Old Fort where displays precede the nightly Sound and Light concerts.

Although a surprising number of the islanders play musical instruments, the bouzouki is not as much in evidence as it once was although it is still played in some tavernas.

FLORA AND FAUNA

Plenty of winter rain, many hours of summer and winter sun and high humidity create growing conditions which are second to none in the Ionian islands and make Corfu so lush and green. Flowers abound in spring from the ubiquitous Spanish broom to rare wild orchids but the best time to see them is from late March through April into May although the season persists longer around the top of Mount Pandokrator. Despite the heat and the lack of water in summer, there is always a few flowers to be seen, like the beautiful sea daffodil, Pancratium maritimum, and the mulleins. Autumn rains bring out the crocus and cyclamen in a new flush of flowers which help to keep winter colourful until spring gets into its stride once again.

Bird watchers will not be disap-pointed either since the island has a wide variety of habitats from sea cliffs to marshes and lakes. Some of the more colourful species include bee-eaters, golden orioles, hoopoes, rollers and kingfishers.

The fauna is surprisingly good too and the island has a wide range of wild animals including foxes, hares, weasels, pine martins and hedgehogs. The latter is the one most likely to be seen since so many fail to cross the road safely. It is said that the nocturnal jackal still exists on the island but sightings are few. Tortoises are around in great numbers and these too are often seen on the road. Greek drivers believe it unlucky to run over a tortoise so they go to great lengths to avoid them. Fireflies are one of the delights in store for the May visitor, as darkness descends they set up their own spectacular displays in search of mates. Brilliant specs of light flash away beneath the trees and along the dark roadways.

Snakes are around too in numbers but mostly harmless. There is one poisonous viper species, Viper ammodytes, which is mostly nocturnal and unlikely to be encountered.

HOLIDAY READING

There is no greater pleasure than reading a book in the location where the book is set, especially when the period is different. *My Family and Other Animals* by Gerald Durell which delighted millions as a television adaptation is set on Corfu. His brother Lawrence's book, *Prospero's Cell* gives a deeper insight into Corfiot life at the same period and millenniums earlier is Homer's *Odyssey*. Modern translations of this are in narrative form and read like a novel.

A LITTLE LIGHT HISTORY

Man was around this island enjoying its high fertility and good climate as early as prehistoric times leaving rich traces of archaeological evidence. Little is known of these early times and the island's history only comes into focus with the arrival of settlers from Corinth in 734BC.

They were not the first colonists, others had arrived from Eritrea around 775-750BC but these were quickly eclipsed by the Corinthians.

Corinth, around this period, had grown into a mercantile power enjoying unrivalled prosperity. Nothing attracts more than success and it soon found its population growing beyond its bounds so it set about forming colonies. Corfu was one chosen site as was Syracuse (Sicily). Both these colonies quickly started to flourish in their own right.

The Birth of Kerkyra (Corfu)

Settlement in Corfu took place around the neck of the Kanoni peninsula, just south of the present Corfu town, to take advantage of the harbours on either side. Here a new city sprang up known as Korkyra which was to give the island its modern name, Kerkyra. The city prospered and expanded as the settlement became an important trading post in its own right. There are still some ancient remains to visit in this area which are described in more detail in a later tour. (see page 60). Corfu's strategic position between the Adriatic coastal ports and Corinth guaranteed its success and it soon grew wealthy and powerful. From the early sixth century BC it started to mint its own coins and its naval strength grew to become one of the largest in the Greek world, second only to Athens. Relations with Corinth remained good in the early years. They co-operated to form new colonies at Epidamos (Albania) and Illyria (Adriatic coast) but in 435BC squabbles started over the joint colony of Edpidamos which was promptly taken over by Corinth. Resentment on Korkyra ran high so they assembled a naval blockade of forty ships around Epidamos to force its surrender. Corinth, none too pleased, responded by sending a squadron of 75 ships and 2,000 hoplites against Korkyra. Without loosening its grip on Epidamos, the remaining eighty ships of Corfu were able to win a convincing victory over the Cor-inthians. Damaged but by no means destroyed, Corinth prepared for an even larger assault by building more ships and calling on the Peloponnesian League for

Flowers on Corfu

Corfu is prolific with flowers during the months of spring

Above: Allium Roseum

Below: Oleander

Above, left: Orchis Quadripunctata, and right: Orchis Provincialis

Below, left: Orchis Tridentata, and right: Serapias Orientalis

support. With no one else to turn to, Korkyra look-ed to Athens for support and so Greece slid into the devastating Peloponnesian War which raged for 27 years.

An Island in Decline

In retrospect, the Peloponnesian War was probably a turning point in the island's fortunes, mainly because it marked the beginning of the decline of the powerful Athenian empire. Korkyra emerged from the war with a strong navy and still in league with Athens but the alliance was not to hold for much longer. In 375BC the island was still strong enough to fight off the territorial ambitions of the Spartans and join Athens in 338BC fighting Philip of Macedon. By the end of the fourth century the island fell to the Spart-ans. Strategically placed and highly desirable Korkyra had several masters in quick succession and was further weakened by plundering Illy-rian pirates. In 229BC the island was handed over to the Romans and had the distinction of becoming Rome's first Greek dependency.

Under the Romans

From 229BC to AD337, Corfu enjoyed a period of relative tranquillity and prosperity under the benign rule of the Romans. A powerful Roman fleet was based there and the island granted many privileges. Christianity arrived late in the first century with Jason and Sosipater, disciples of St Paul, who were later canonised.

The Byzantine Period (AD337-1267)

In AD337, when the massive Roman Empire was divided into two, Corfu was included in the eastern section which later became the Byzantine Empire. Around this period in history, Barbarian tribes from Europe, namely the Vandals and the Goths, were worrying the Roman Empire and from the fifth to the seventh centuries Corfu suffered heavily in raiding expeditions. The Muslim Saracens too mounted raids from North Africa. After one particularly destructive raid by the Goths in 562 which effectively destroyed the capital, the island was stirred to build a fort (the Old Fort) for its protection which became the nucleus of the new town and coastal settlements moved inland to hide in the mountains.

From the eighth century onwards, Corfu was under the administration (thema) of Kefalonia and in 876 the Church of Corfu became an archbishopric (metropolis) under the Patriarch of Constantinople. By the eleventh century, events and a changing situation in Europe posed new threats to Corfu, especially with its exposed location at the extreme western edge of the Byzantine Empire. The Normans were busy pushing into this part of the world and in 1081 they occupied Corfu but only for three years until it was regained by the Byzantines with the aid of the now powerful Venice. In return the Venetians were granted trading privileges. There was to be no lasting peace, the island was attacked again and again during the twelfth century firstly by the Normans and then the Genoese. The Byzantine Empire finally crumbled as a result of the Fourth Crusade (1202-4). Thanks to help offered to the Crusaders, the Venetians gained control of a number of territories along its trade route to the Levant which included the Ionian islands although it was 1206 before it was able to secure Corfu from the control of the Genoese.

The House of Anjou (1267-1386)

Still prized for its strategic position, Corfu was to remain a pawn in a power battle over the next century and a half. After the disintegration of Byzantium, Epirus, the mainland opposite Corfu, became an independent Greek state ruled by Michael I Angelos who, in 1214, seized the islands from the Venetians. It was he who built the castles of Angelokastro near Paleokastritsa and Gardiki in the south. Later, in 1257, Corfu was used as a dowry and given away on the marriage of Helena, daughter of Michael II Angelos, to Manfred, King of the Two Sicilies. Manfred came into conflict with the Pope who responded

by supporting Charles, Duke of Anjou, in his bid to capture the Kingdom of the two Sicilies. The two met in battle and Manfred was killed which allowed Charles, in 1267, to take control of Corfu.

Life became much harder on the island as Charles of Anjou took away religious freedom and forcibly imposed Catholicism. The system of administration was changed to match feudal Europe but, while the rule was harsh, it produced a period of prosperity and stability which lasted until the House of Anjou itself went into decline.

Under the Venetians (1386-1797)

When the Venetians moved in to take the prize they had always coveted, the island greeted them as liberators. The existing feudal system and aristocracy were not just maintained but reinforced by the Venetians who were also intent on rebuilding and strengthening the fortifications. Olive trees were introduced in vast numbers for the production of oil and to the detriment of other crops, like grain. The peasants were tied to land which did not belong to them and treated as serfs with no education and very little freedom. In contrast the burgher class, mainly merchants, were granted privileges and many were able to amass wealth. Thanks to the tolerance of the Venetians, Greek Orthodoxy made something of a return in

Following Page: Loading a donkey at Marmaro

Above: Mora'i'tika is an emerging resort with a nice beach of sand and shingle

this period much to the dismay of the Catholic clergy.

These were not peaceful times for the island. Venice was in constant running battles with the Turks who, by 1453, occupied much of mainland Greece and were intent on swallowing up the islands. Although Venice had lost ground to the Turks on the mainland, it was determined to hold on to the Ionian Islands and, with the help of the Corfiot people, it resisted the Turks successfully in 1451 but less so in 1537 when Barbarossa landed on the island with a force of 25,000 men. They pillaged the island, killed or captured as many as 20,000 Corfiots, laid siege to the main town but retired after two weeks. Realising the need for still more defences, a canal was cut to further isolate the Old Fort and the New Fort was started. To ease the problems of depopulation Greeks were brought in from other areas and privileges granted to encourage them to settle but there was a steady influx of refugees from regions taken over by the Turks.

The Turkish menace continued with further forays against the island in the rest of the sixteenth century. Corfu was considerably strengthened by a large influx of Greek refugees following the fall of Crete to the Turks in 1669. Now the Venetians most important overseas possession, the defence of the island was put into the hands of the Austrian, Hans Matthias von der Schulenburg who prepared well to resist what proved to be the final and most determined attack by the Turks in 1716. Some 30,000 Turks were landed on the island but they were resisted and fled on 11 August after a great storm and the rumour that the island's patron saint, Ag. Spiridon, had appeared. Exhausted by the long struggle, Venice went into serious decline until it was finally defeated by Napoleon when Corfu became a French possession.

Visitors to Corfu can see for themselves the legacy of the Venetian rule in the tall buildings of Corfu town, the arcaded streets and the old fort.

A thousand years of Byzantine rule had left virtually no imprint on the island. Conversely, four hundred years under the Venetians shaped the character of the island both in its architecture and cultural expression. Corfu town is full of typical Venetian style tall houses, narrow streets and arcaded walkways, the Old Fort is Venetian and even the theatre is a cultural legacy.

French and Russian Masters (1797-1814)

Like they did with the Venetians four hundred years earlier, the Corfiots greeted the French as liberators and busied themselves destroying the emblems of the Venetians. However, the French rapidly made themselves unpopular by confiscation of property and raising new taxes. After only two years, when the island came under siege from the Russo-Turkish alliance, the French were in trouble. Having lost the support of the Corfiots, the French soon capitulated and were despatched from the island after a war lasting only four months.

The Turkish and Russian admirals made a joint declaration that the Ionian islands were to become one nation, the Septinsular Republic. Fourteen delegates from the islands made up the governing senate and eventually a constitution was drawn up in which it was forced to recognise the fact that the Republic was a Russian protectorate. To the delight of the people, the Russians restored the full rights of the Greek Orthodox church.

There was still no settled existence or master for, under the Treaty of Tilsit in 1807, Corfu was ceded back to the French. At least in their second period of occupation, the French were more benevolent. This was the period in which the elegant arcades of the Liston were built along the Esplanade and in which an

Ionian Academy was opened to promote science along with arts and crafts. The French rule came to an abrupt end in 1815 with the abdication of Napoleon after the Battle of Waterloo.

Under the British (1815-1864)

The Treaty of Paris in 1815 decreed that the United States of the Ionian islands should become a protectorate of the British. Sir Thomas Maitland, the first Lord High Commissioner, proved to be autocratic. He took the view that the island was not ready for democratic rule so he devised a constitution which gave him firm control. As a Senate House, and his own personal palace, he built the Palace of St Michael and St John. On the more positive side he introduced a vigorous road building programme which opened up the island to wheeled traffic, improved the infrastructure and built hospitals.

On the mainland, there was a struggle in progress by 1821 to overthrow Turkish rule and the Corfiot John Kapodistrias (who later became the first president of Greece and was assassinated in 1831) pressed the British to allow Corfu to help but to no avail. This decision did nothing to win over the Corfiots who were generally resentful of the British rule.

Sir Frederick Adam, who succeeded to Lord High Commissioner, won over the islanders perhaps more than any other. It was he who brought water to Corfu town by building an aqueduct from Benitses. Reform continued slowly and a revised constitution in 1848 recognised freedom of the press and with it the recognition that there was growing support for union with Greece.

The period of British rule had many positive aspects. It saw the abolition of fiefs by law, improved living standards, an improved level of education and a general increase in prosperity.

Union with Greece (1864)

Corfu, along with the other Ionian islands, were ceded to Greece as a gesture of goodwill when the British-backed Prince William of Denmark became King George I of Hellenes. Part of the conditions were that Corfu remained perpetually neutral.

In spite of its neutrality, Corfu was still drawn into the troubled events of the twentieth century. It was used as a base by the British, French and Italian Allied forces in World War I. In the World War II, Corfu was occupied by the Italians in 1941 who planned once again to establish a separate Ionian State. It was not to be for, following the Anglo-Italian armistice in 1943, the Germans launched an attack to capture the island. The bombardment lasted ten days and inflicted massive damage on Corfu town destroying many important buildings. In the following year Corfu was finally liberated by the Allied forces.

Out and About

Good Beach Guide

A day out on a different beach provides a refreshing change and the purpose of this Good Beach Guide is to help with choices. It is not intended to be a comprehensive list but includes only those beaches with good features which reward the effort of getting there. Sandy beaches have been selected in the main but outstandingly good shingle beaches are also listed. Refer to the map on pages 22/23 for locations and for ease of reference they are listed in clockwise order starting from Corfu town. In some cases more details may be found by consulting the appropriate car tour.

As a broad general pointer, scenic beaches with good quality sand are mostly found on the western coasts where the sea is often rougher whilst the north coast loses something in scenery but still has good sandy beaches. The east coast has to make do mostly with shingle but mostly calm seas. Again in general terms, good sand and shallow seas suitable for families are found mostly along the north coast. There are plenty of lively beaches and quieter beaches too but isolated beaches for skinny dipping are harder to find since Corfu is now a mature tourist destination and there is barely a corner not discovered.

Mora'i'tika: Beach fairly narrow, mainly sand with some shingle and away from the main road. Plenty of facilities for snacks and drinks, plenty of water sports. Moderately busy in season.

Kavos: Wonderful stretch of sand in scenic location with safe bathing for children but this is a swinging beach; the beat of music never far away, plenty of water sports and busy with the young set. Full facilities, expect it to be crowded at any time in the season.

Ag Georgios (south): fine, sandy beach backed by low cliffs. There are actually two beaches separated by a headland with the north beach more popular. On the quiet side but there are enough facilities including some water sports and it is good for families.

Ag Gordis: Very scenic, large sandy beach nestling beneath wooded cliffs. Plenty of beach side tavernas and cafes, water sports and good for families although sea sometimes rough along this coast. Moderately busy, very limited parking.

Pelekas Beach: A lovely crescent of fine sand in attractive setting. For access follow signs to Yaliskari Palace Hotel and continue past, park above the beach and walk down the steep track. Sun loungers and umbrellas available, some facilities but one of the quieter beaches.

Preceding page: The Esplanade looking towards the Palace and the Cricket ground

Glifada Beach: A long, deep stretch of golden sand in picturesque setting. Cafés, bars and tavernas on hand and plenty of water sports available. Good for families except when the sea is rough. Very popular with day visitors in main season. Some parking available.

Paleokastritsa: one of the islands top beauty spots. Attractive bay of sand/shingle with all facilities including water sports. Very busy with day trippers for much of the season.

Ag Georgiou (north): A golden sandy beach with plenty of character. Not especially easy to reach but served by buses from Corfu town. Plenty of facilities including water sports but not too crowded.

Sidari: plenty of beach space to absorb the crowds. Especially good for children with warm shallow seas. Swimmers will find more satisfaction in the bays at the western edge of the resort. Full facilities.

Roda: another good, safe beach for children, fairly busy and with good support facilities.

Acharavi: a continuation of Roda beach and similar in character.

Barbati Beach: White shingle beach in spectacular setting, sun loungers and umbrellas, water sports and enough facilities to survive happily. On the quiet side.

A DAY IN CORFU TOWN

The two fortresses guarding old Corfu (Kerkyra) town may have held back earlier invaders but the tide of tourism is unstoppable. Its magnetism is due in no small part to a Venetian atmosphere which still pervades the elegant arcades and maze of bustling narrow streets. Here, it is possible to admire the architecture, indulge a passion for shopping or relax in one of the many small intimate squares. Within a relatively compact area lie a wealth of things to see and do from markets, museums, churches and even a cricket match on the Esplanade. The peaceful garden ambience of the British cemetery provides an unusual but welcome retreat and insight into the history of the British on Corfu. It also draws many visitors to admire the magnificent spring display of wild orchids. A popular pastime, is to take time out and enjoy a different perspective of the old town from a colourful horse-drawn landau. These tout for custom outside the entrance to the old fort.

A one day visit should cover the main points of interest which are the old and new fortresses, Esplanade, Liston building, Palace, Orthodox Cathedral, Church of St Spiridon, Archaeological Museum and the Old Town (Campiello Quarter). More time is needed to absorb the atmosphere and seek out more of what the town has to offer.

The **Esplanade**, or Spianada to the Greeks, is the hub of Corfiot so-

Sunseeker Tips

1. BEACH SAFETY
A flag system operates on many of the popular beaches to advise on the bathing conditions.
A red flag flying means that conditions are unsuitable for water sports.
A yellow flag indicates that water sports may be dangerous.
A dark green flag indicates conditions are fine.
A black flag bans swimming.

2. BEACH BEDS
The cost of hiring sun beds and umbrellas is overpriced and seems to climb each year. The total cost over a full two week holiday can be quite significant. A full day's rate is charged even if the loungers are used for only a couple of hours. One alternative is to buy beach umbrellas and air beds which are freely available in the shops. Their cost will be recovered in just two or three days and, if luggage space is tight when departing, it is no loss if they are passed on to some newly arrived holidaymakers.

3. BARS WITH POOLS
Watch out for one of the growing number of purpose built bars with swimming pools which offer all the facilities free to customers, including free use of sun beds and parasols, providing drinks and food are bought from the bar. Prices are not usually elevated and many of these sell good value bar snacks. It is a growing market and a number of hotels are following the trend and also offer their swimming pool and facilities free on the same basis.

4. FRAPPE
Hot drinks lose their appeal when the weather is very hot and a more suitable drink for coffee fans is iced coffee or frappe. It is very easy to make and self catering visitors can put one together in a trice. Plastic frappe makers, nothing more than a plastic container with lid, can be bought cheaply but an empty coffee jar with lid is ideal. For one cup add a normal measure of instant coffee, ice cubes, milk and sugar if taken, and a cup of chilled water. Shake vigorously to dissolve the coffee, around 30 seconds, pour into a glass and it should have a good head of froth. Drink through a straw, for some reason it tastes better.

5. POST CARDS
To speed up the delivery of postcards, put them into an airmail envelope before posting. Postal rate is the same and they are delivered as letters which means a few days instead of a couple of weeks. Envelopes (*fakellos*) can be bought cheaply at stationers.

6. MUSEUMS AND ARCHAEOLOGICAL SITES
Except for private museums, they are all free entrance on Sunday throughout Greece.

A Note of Warning
Care is needed on the beach to avoid stings from jelly fish and, in rocky regions, from sea urchins. If you are unlucky enough to have a brush with the latter then it is important to ensure that all the spines are properly removed. Wearing beach shoes will give your feet some protection from stings of this nature (see also Mosquitoes, page 126).

cial life. This vast open space of parkland was cleared of buildings by the Venetians in 1537, as a defence measure when the Turks first turned their attention on Corfu. Afterwards used as a parade ground it was transformed into gardens during the French occupation. The elegant arcaded **Liston building**, overlooking the cricket ground, stems from this era and was designed by the French governor of the island Mathieu de Lesseps whose son Ferdinand built the Suez Canal. Lesseps based the design on similar arcades in the Rue de Rivoli in Paris. Started in 1807, it took fifteen years to complete. The name Liston evolved from the 'list' of noble families who were allowed exclusive use of the arcades. Now, its cafés are a focal point for the evening 'volta' where locals come to see and be seen in all their finery. Shaded tables under the trees also provide a comfortable vantage point from where to watch local and occasional overseas teams play cricket, a game introduced by the British and now firmly established on the island. Close to the junction of Doumani and Kapodistriou are some beautifully appointed state of the art WCs. A puzzle being the high-tech extraction of soap and water to wash your hands.

Amongst the monuments which adorn the Esplanade are: the **Schulenburg Memorial** (near the old fort entrance) dedicated to a German mercenary, Count Johann Matthias der Schulenburg, who in 1716 successfully helped the Venetians repel an attack by the Turks; the

Maitland Rotunda — a memorial to Sir Thomas Maitland who, during his term of office as Lord High Commissioner of the Ionian Islands 1816-1824, gave the island an infrastructure of roads and sanitation; the **Ionian Monument** — to commemorate 21 May 1864 when the Ionian Islands were united with independent Greece; the **Kapodistrias Memorial** — to the Corfiot Yannis Kapodistrias who was the first leader of independent Greece from 1827-1831. He is buried in the grounds of the Platitera Monastery on the outskirts of town.

Palace of St Michael and St George — built between 1818 and 1823 by the English architect Sir George Whitmore, for the British governors of Corfu. Besides being a residence, it also served as the seat of the Ionian Parliament and Treasury of the new Order of SS Michael and George, instigated in 1818 to reward Britons whose service to the crown in Malta and the Ionian Island Union warranted merit. The first British Lord High Commissioner, Sir Thomas Maitland or 'King Tom', was also Governor of Malta, which explains why Maltese limestone and stonemasons came to be used in its construction. This charming Regency, neo-classical building, with a Doric portico which links triumphal arched gates and pavilions at either end, is the oldest official building in modern Greece. A frieze along the façade depicts the emblems of the seven Ionian islands, a detail also found on the Maitland Memorial. The toga-clad statue in front of the Palace is that of the second High Commissioner, Sir Frederick Adam, who built Mon Repos and gave the town its water system. When the British left Corfu in 1864, the Palace became a Greek royal residence. Within the Palace is the Museum of Asiatic Art, the only one of its kind in Greece. This is a stunning collection of Chinese, Japanese and Indian art from the Neolithic era through to the nineteenth century, donated by private individuals. Due to ongoing renovation work, access to the Palace and Museum may be restricted.

Between the Palace and Old Fort is the small **church of Panagia Mandrakini**, which overlooks Mandraki harbour, and a statue to Frederick North, Fifth Earl of Guilford (1769-1828). He brought prominence to Corfu by founding the first seat of higher education in modern Greece, a New Ionian Academy.

Old Fort (Paleo Frourio) — is on the two-peaked promontory chosen by the citizens of ancient Paleopolis (on Kanoni), in the sixth century, to found a new settlement. As defence against persistent barbarian raids, the Byzantines fortified the eastern peak but defensive building developed apace under the Venetians against the constant threat of Turkish attack. They fortified the western peak and in the sixteenth century dug a moat, the 'contrafossa', effectively separating the fort from the mainland. The Venetian name for the island, Corfu, was a derivation of Korypho, the Byzantine name for the twin-peaked promontory. With the arrival of the British, the Venetian buildings inside the fort were replaced with barracks and a military hospital. Extensive damage to the fortifications was inflicted by two massive explosions in the powder magazine in 1718 and 1789 and later German bombing raids during World War II. Recent renovation has transformed the interior, especially the garrison church of St George, built in 1830 in the style of a Doric temple. It is now used as a venue for some excellent travelling exhibitions. Entrance is across the sixteenth-century Venetian moat, the 'contrafossa', and there are clean, modern WCs immediately to the right. Beyond and right leads to the Doric style church whilst left leads to the 'Sound and Light' show venue and sailing club harbour of Mandraki. Here is where the Venetian war galleys were moored, some of the mooring posts still visible. Superb views over the town and island can be enjoyed from the lighthouse. It is approached along a paved path which initially heads up to the clock tower past a Venetian cistern.

Open: Tuesday to Friday 8am-7pm; Saturday, Sunday and holidays 8.30am - 3.00pm; closed Monday. Admission charge.

This next part of the walk actually skirts round three sides of the Campiello quarter. North from the Esplanade leads past the distinctive **Corfu Reading Society building** with its exterior stairway, founded by the British in 1836. The sixteenth-century sea gate of St Nicholas lies down the ramp to the right as you round the corner into Arseniou.

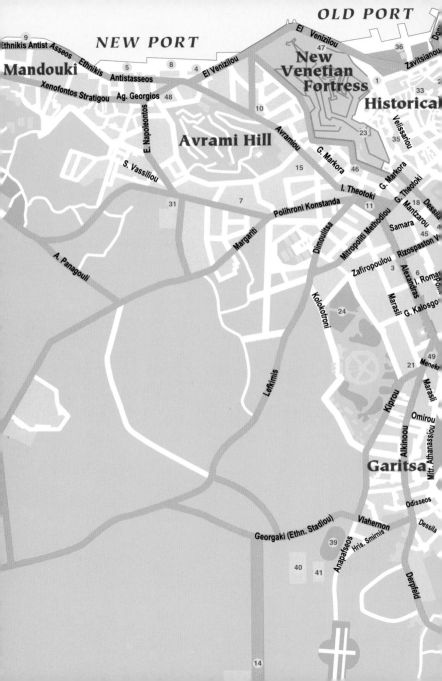

Corfu Town

OLD VENETIAN FORTRESS

1 GNTO-TOURIST POLICE
2 TOWN HALL
3 POST OFFICE
4 TELEPHONE OFFICES (OTE)
5 CUSTOMS
6 POLICE DEPARTMENT
7 HOSPITAL/FIRST AID
8 FORIEGN PASSENGER FERRIES
9 DOMESTIC PASSENGER FERRIES
10 KTEL LONG DISTANCE (GREEN) BUS TERMINAL
11 CITY (BLUE) BUS TERMINAL
12 BUSES FOR KANONI
13 OLYMPIC AIRLINES
14 AIRPORT
15 UNIVERSITY
16 IONIAN ACADEMY
17 READING SOCIETY
18 MUNICIPAL THEATRE
19 SOUND AND LIGHT
20 PALEOPOLIS
21 TOMB OF MENEKRATES
22 OLD FORT
23 NEW FORT
24 ENGLISH CEMETERY
25 PALACE
26 ARCHAEOLOGICAL MUSEUM

CORFU SHELL MUSEUM
BYZANTINE MUSEUM
27 STS. JASON AND SOSIPATER (BYZANTINE)
28 AGIA THEODORA AUGUSTA (GREEK ORTHODOX CATHEDRAL)
29 AGIOS SPYRIDON
30 AGIOS GEORGIOS
31 PLATITERA MONASTERY
32 AGIOS CHRISTOFOROS (GREEK CATHOLIC CATHEDRAL)
33 AGIOS FRANKISKOS (ROMAN CATHOLIC)
34 HOLY TRINITY (ANGLICAN)
35 SYNAGOGUE
36 ELPA (HELLENIC AUTOMOBILE AND TOURING ASSOCIATION)
37 CORFU YACHT CLUB
38 OPEN SEA SAILING CLUB
39 STADIUM
40 PUBLIC SWIMMING POOL
41 INDOOR COURTS
42 TENNIS COURTS
43 CRICKET GROUND
44 CORFU PALACE (HOTEL)
45 TOURIST OFFICE
46 MARKETS
47 CAR HIRE

CONSULATES
48 DENMARK
49 GREAT BRITAIN
50 IRELAND
51 NETHERLANDS
52 NORWAY
53 SWEDEN

Tavernas here, along the top of the sea wall, provide a good viewpoint over to Vidos island close-by. Once forested Vidos was variously used as a hunting ground, then as a battery by attacking Turkish forces before the British dismantled its fortifications and it became a penal settlement. Exiled Serbians were also contained there when they fled to Corfu during World War I. Today it has reverted to being a local beauty spot, accessible by boat from the Old Port. To the left, steps lead up to the **Byzantine Museum** in the church of Panagia Antivouniotissa. The ikons on display date from the thirteenth to the seventeenth centuries and include some found fairly recently in the church of St George in the Old Fortress.

Open: Tuesday to Sunday; closed Monday. Admission charge.

Close by is the **Solomos Museum**. Greece's national poet Dionysos Solomos, from Zakynthos, lived in this house from 1828 until his death in 1857. The first two stanzas of his poem, 'Hymn to Freedom', was set to music and became the Greek national anthem. This collection of memorabilia is of little interest to non-Greeks unless able to read Greek.

Open: Monday to Friday 6-9pm. Free admission.

Head down Donzelot to George II Square the Old Port and the Spilia gate into the old town. On the far side looms the New Fortress beyond which lies the New Port area. To find the entrance to the fort, cross Solomou Square and go right up Solomou following the signs. The entrance is to the right before entering the tunnel through the walls.

The **New Fortress** (Neo Frourio) — the Turkish siege of 1537 highlighted the vulnerability of the small overspill settlement which had developed outside the walls of the Old Fortress but, it was to take over thirty years before work commenced on the New Fortress. Although access is restricted, as part of the fort is still used by the Greek Navy, there are an intriguing number of passageways to explore. The fantastic views alone over the well-worn mellow, ochre tiled rooftops of old Corfu town and beyond to mainland Greece and Albania make a visit worthwhile. Inside, there is a small café, gallery and museum shop where replicas of statuary are on sale.

Open: Seven days a week including holidays 9am-7pm. Admission charge.

From the New Fortress continue right through the tunnel in the wall. Emerge onto the road which was once the line of the moat and turn left. Right heads back to the sea and the New Port area. Along here are located the fruit and vegetable and fish markets. At the junction with G.Theotoki turn left to head back into the old town. Keep ahead into **Voulgareos** known for its silversmiths. To the north is the old ghetto area and Corfu's only remaining synagogue. A good bookshop, for guides and maps in English, can be found in M.Theotoki Square along with a selection of banks. The section of Voulgareos beyond the square, which leads back to the Esplanade, is lined with upmarket shoe boutiques and jewellery shops. To the right off here, fronting a particularly attractive sloping square, is the **Town Hall**. White marble from Sinies on Mount Pandokrator was hewn for its construction in 1663. Initially used as an assembly room for the nobility, it became the San Giacomo Theatre in 1720 until further change to an opera house. Italian opera companies regularly toured the Ionian islands whose inhabitants had a passion for opera. On completion of a new theatre, a second storey was added and in 1903 the building reverted to its present role.

North of the Town Hall leads into the maze which is the very heart of the old town. Here, a different cameo awaits around every corner where the crumbling façades of tall buildings, arcades which offer shelter from the sun or rain, green shutters, flowers, flapping washing and fascinating, tucked out of the way, miniature squares exude an enchanting air of faded elegance. Seek out the beautiful Venetian wellhead from 1699 in **Kremasti Square**, not far from the Orthodox Cathedral. In this area lie two of Corfu's most important churches and the unusual **Paper Money Museum**, housed in the Ionian Bank building off N.Theotoki. Besides a comprehensive display of Greek notes from 1820 and foreign notes, the design and production of a note is exhibited. Open: Monday to Saturday 9am-1pm; closed Sunday. Free admission.

The **Church of St Spiridon** (Ag Spiridonos), on the street of the same name behind the Liston building, has an ochre coloured reddish brown capped bell-tower which is the tallest on the island. Built especially to house the mummified remains of Spiridon, the island's patron saint, in 1590, the church bulges at the seams with silver chandeliers and incense burners not to mention valuable ikons. A silver casket contains the saint's body in a chapel to the right of the altar. The body is paraded round the town four times yearly on Palm Sunday, Easter Saturday, 11 August and the first Sunday in November, a glass fronted panel in the gilt casket used for this occasion allowing sight of his shrivelled face. His name day on 12 December is shared by the many Spiro's amongst the male population on Corfu. On this day, the faithful flock to kiss the slippered feet of the saint who has saved them from many disasters down the centuries.

The **Greek Orthodox Cathedral of Panagia Spiliotissa** (Madonna of the Cave) is off Ag Theodoras and where the headless remains of St Theodora are preserved in a silver casket. She is revered as the island's second saint and her casket opened once a year. The church dates from 1577 but only acquired cathedral status in 1841.

Within walking distance south of the town centre lie the remaining points of interest.

Archaeological Museum — this pleasant museum is only a short walk south from the Esplanade and a right turn up Vraila, just past the

Saints Spiridon and Theodora

S t Spiridon was a Cypriot shepherd from Trimithion, near Nicosia, who became a priest. He rose to the post of a minor bishop who in AD325 attended the Council of Nicaea which formally lay down a summary of Christian beliefs (Nicene Creed). Many miracles were attributed to him during his lifetime. After his death, a sweet odour rising from his grave prompted exhumation when he was found to be in a perfect state of preservation. Elevated to sainthood, his remains were eventually removed to Constantinople to protect them from Saracen raids. Here, St Spiridon's remains along with those of St Theodora Augusta, came into the possession of a wealthy priest, Kalocheiritis. St Theodora was a ninth-century Byzantine empress who was instrumental in the restoration of ikon worship which had been in danger of being banned. Kalocheiritis made a timely exit from Constantinople in 1453, just before the Turks captured the city, travelling through Epirus to Corfu with his charges in straw filled sacks slung on the back of a mule.

The body of St Theodora was donated to the community whilst that of St Spiridon remained in the priest's family until placed in its own church.

Below: The arches of the Liston building are based on the design of the Rue de Rivoli in Paris

Above: The Panagia Mandrakini chapel

Best Buys

The greatest concentration of shops lies in Corfu town but workshops for wood, pottery and leather are scattered around the island.

Gold and silver are good buys and the prices are keener than can normally be obtained in Europe. Jewellery designs are based on traditional motifs that have survived from Minoan times and also reflect Byzantine and Venetian influences.

Olive wood carving is very popular on Corfu and there are a number of workshops and shops dedicated to these products.

Kumquat is a liqueur unique to the island and it is available in several styles. This is your only chance to buy it. (See page 84).

The local honey is excellent and the best place to buy is from local stalls when travelling around the island.

Leather and lace work are also good buys. Save buying lace until Kassiopi is visited.

Corfou Palace Hotel. The main at-traction of the museum is the 2,500 year old 'Gorgon Pediment'; the old-est surviving monumental sculpture in Greece, which shows Medusa with her children Pegasus and Chrysaor. It was unearthed in 1912 from the site of the sixth-century Temple of Artemis, near the airport, within the boundary of the ancient city of Paleopolis (Korcyra). Other finds from Paleopolis include a Corinthian statue of a crouching lion, found near the tomb of Mene-krates, and a collection of interesting artefacts from sites scattered around the island; all well displayed and with English translations.

Open: daily including Sunday and holidays 8.30am-3pm; closed Monday. Admission charge.

⛩ **Tomb of Menekrates** — at the top of Menekratous, further south than the Archaeological Museum. A cir-cular tomb with a conical roof from around 600BC which stands on the site of the extensive ancient nek-ropolis of Paleopolis.

✳ **British Cemetery** — located in an unbelievably peaceful setting reach-ed by heading up Marasli from the Tomb of Menekrates. A left into Zafiropoulo and a further left down Kolokotroni leads directly to the en-trance. Enter by the small gate to the right of the double gates. The genial caretaker is George Psaila, a British citizen. He usually appears for a chat but leaves visitors to wander freely in this park-like enclave.

Open: daily, all day.

A quick return to the centre is straight along Mitropoliti Meth-odiou, through San Rocco Square (G.Theotoki Square), once an outly-ing village, and on down G. Theo-toki. The Theotoki family influence on Corfiot life tells its own tale in the number of streets named for them. Fleeing to Corfu when Constantino-ple fell to the Turks in 1453, the fam-ily pro-duced a succession of suc-cessful landowners and statesmen.

A HALF-DAY VISIT TO KANONI (ANCIENT KORCYRA/PALEOPOLIS)

Kanoni is a picturesque wooded pe-ninsula and the location of ancient Paleopolis (Korcyra). The walls of ⛩ the ancient city once stretched across the neck of the peninsula between the harbours of Alkinoos and Hyll-aikos. Some of Corfu's major hotels are located here and it is still re-garded as a choice suburb, despite its proximity to the airport. On the plus side, the area still retains pockets of the idyllic charm which has tempted day trippers out from Corfu Town for the past two hundred years. Kanoni gets its name from the can-non placed at the end of the penin-sula by the French, to protect the Chalikopoulos lagoon. Nowadays, the cannon is barely given a second glance. Its vantage point looks over the main attractions, the islands of Vlacherna and Pontikonissi (Mouse Island).

This trip can be accomplished on foot, by car or by local bus from the Esplanade to the end of the penin-sula overlooking Mouse island and walk back. Parking difficulties can be expected by car. Highlights include: Mon Repos and its gardens; the tiny monastery of Ag Efthimeas; the fifth-century basilica of Ag Kerkyra; ruins of the Doric temple of Artemis; various remains of old Paleopolis; Mouse island.

Follow the promenade south round Garitsa Bay along Dimokratias, which skirts the suburb of Garitsa — once village of Kastrades, then follow signs for Kanoni up Nafsikas. To the left is the suburb of Anemomilos on land which was once ancient Alkinoos harbour. Excavations along Nafsikas have revealed foundations of harbour buildings. (The airport runway now slices across the ancient city's other harbour, Hyllaikos.) Close by to the left can be found the only genuine **Byzantine church** on Corfu, built in the eleventh century and dedicated to SS Jason and Sosipater. As disciples of St Paul they brought Christianity to the island during the Roman era, but were brutally martyred. Some of ancient Paleopolis can be detected in the building materials used and there are remains of frescos.

Open: most days from 8.30am to 10.30pm.

On meeting E.Theotoki, keep right and look for a narrow road rising left signposted to **Moni Ag Efthimeas** (1862). A pretty little nunnery with white cloisters enclosing a small flower and vine filled garden. Open: 8am-1pm and 5-8.00pm. Shortly after the turn up to the monastery you reach a crossroads. The noticeable ruin to the right is the fifth-century **Basilica of Ag Kerkyra**, also known as Paleopolis Church. Options for searching out the remains of Paleopolis start here. To the left are the gates into Mon Repos whose grounds cover much of the ancient city. The road left leads up to Analipsis, site of the Acropolis, and right to the Temple of Artemis.

Mon Repos — was built for the second British Commissioner Sir Frederick Adam in 1824. It later became the summer residence of the Greek royal family and was the birthplace of Prince Philip, Duke of Edinburgh. Wander up the drive through neglected grounds which were once home to the Ionian Academy's Botanical Gardens. The villa lies shuttered and in a sad state of repair at present. Signs indicate the onward route to the site of the ancient temples of Apollo and Hera, which are not too far from a lodge distinguished by a porch with an unusual spired roof. Limited excavations so far reveal a section of wall and fragments of ribbed columns.

Open: 8am-6pm.

For the hamlet of **Analipsis** (Ascension) and the site of the **Acropolis of Paleopolis**, take the road up left beside Mon Repos. Go left at the T junction and keep on to the top. Head for the small white **church of Ag Marina** (1892), on the hilltop to the left, which is a magnificent viewpoint. A path leads down, skirting Mon Repos over left, to **Kardaki Spring**. According to local legend, he who drinks the water will never return to his native land.

Above: Contrafossa (moat), and the old fort

Below: British cannon in the old fort

Above: A pleasant way to discover Corfu town is by horse-drawn carriage

Below: The old quarter of the town

To find the **Doric Temple of Artemis**, a ten minute walk, take the road opposite Mon Repos gates with Ag Kerkyra on the left. Turn left at the next turning and keep ahead to **Moni Ag Theodoros**. The nuns welcome visitors between the hours of 9am and 1pm and 5-8pm. Next door, by the roadside, lie the foundations of the sixth-century BC **Temple of Artemis** where the Gorgon pediment was unearthed in 1912 but there is little above ground height to see. A little way beyond the temple site, almost within touching distance of the airport, are the remnants of a gate tower from Paleopolis. An eleventh-century chapel built into its structure no doubt saved it from plunder for building material.

Ag Kerkyra has endured a chequered history since its construction as a five-aisled basilica in the fifth century. Like the original temples on the site, which supplied much of the building material, this church too was destroyed and rebuilt many times before final destruction by a bomb in 1943. The Romans built a small theatre or odeon here, sometime during the second or first century BC, and covered excavations across the road have revealed the site of a Roman Baths.

From hereon, the road does a one-way loop of almost 6km (4 miles) round the peninsula. Quite a pleasant walk, except during the tourist season when a constant stream of vehicles fights for road space en route to view Mouse Island. Before rising up to round the end of the loop, a road forks right to the lagoon entrance where there is car parking. This diversion is the best option if it is busy, to avoid having to drive the loop again, as there is very limited parking at the viewpoint directly off the loop. A stepped path links the viewpoint and terraced cafes above with the causeway below. This is where to enjoy the best view out over the islands **Vlacherna** and **Ponti-konissi (Mouse Island)**, see the cannon which gave Kanoni its name and a ringside seat to inspect the undercarriages of aircraft landing and departing from Corfu airport. Stark but attractive Vlacherna seems to float on the water, its tiny convent accessible along a small causeway. On the other hand, the verdant island of Pontikonissi with its small white church can only be reached by boat. These sail from the end of the Vlacherna causeway. A large causeway for pedestrians and cyclists, which is actually a water main, stretches across the mouth of the lagoon to Perama.

On the return pass the **Corfu Hilton**, which now hosts the island's Casino, secreted in woodland opposite a selection of tavernas and restaurants which front the road. The narrow road wends its way back to Ag Kerkyra at a higher level than the outward route.

A DAY IN PALEOKASTRITSA

A convolution of six natural bays spectacularly set at the foot of steeply wooded slopes create an area of great natural beauty known as Paleokastritsa. It was a favourite spot of Sir Frederick Adam when he was Lord High Commissioner during the time Corfu was a British Protectorate. Since there was no road to it, he proposed a convalescent home be built there for the military and used that as the excuse. The road was built but the home never materialised. Although a monastery existed on the headland there from as early as 1225, it was not supported by a village immediately nearby. People preferred the safety of Lakones perched high above. Now Paleokastritsa has developed into an untidy modern resort straggling down the steep approach road. Fortunately, as a beauty spot it remains relatively unspoilt and it still draws visitors by the coach load.

The main points of interest and things to do include: the ambience of this natural beauty spot; two main bays, one with a fine sandy beach, for sunbathing and swimming; water sports; a trip on a glass-bottomed boat over the clear blue waters; a boat trip to nearby caves; a visit to the Monastery of Theotokos perched on the headland; a walk up the mountainside on an old mule track to Bella Vista for a spec-tacular birds-eye-view of the area.

Most tour operators on the island offer Paleokastritsa as a destination for a full or half day trip. An organised trip often only provides transport so there is no real advantage unless it is economical or especially convenient. There is a regular bus service from Corfu town with six or more buses daily according to the season and there are boat trips from other nearby resorts. A group of four might find it economical to use a taxi.

Without a birds-eye-view of the area, it is hard to appreciate all the convolutions on this part of the coast. The buses and coaches drop passengers by the main bay below the monastery headland where much of the interest is centred and where most of the activity is to be found in the way of boat trips and water sports. Apart from visting local coves and grottoes, the rock of Kolovri is usually featured since this is identified with the Phaeacian ship of Homer's *Odyssey*. Poseidon, angry with the Phaeacians for returning Odysseus to Ithaka, smacked the returning ship with the palm of his hand and turned it to stone just as it neared the harbour.

There are numerous tavernas and cafés close by. Walking back from here and taking the road on the left leads past the rows of tourists shops selling the usual tourist tatt towards the small, picturesque harbour.

The **Monastery of Theotokos,** which also houses a museum, is reached by walking up the road leading onto the headland. Traffic flow along this narrow road is controlled by lights. Walking up takes only a few minutes but the nimble footed can short cut by taking the old donkey trail reached on the right, by a metal water pipe, just around the first bend. The **museum** is free of charge and open through the summer, from 1 April to 31 October, between 7am-1pm and 3-8pm. Sensible

Above: Paleokastritsa, the coast to the east

Below, left: Part of the harbour, and right: The monastery bell tower

Above: The beach beyond the carpark

Below, left: The coast north of the monastery

dress is requested which here means no swimming costumes. In some churches and monasteries shorts are unacceptable but here they seem more relaxed. A monastery has existed on this spot since 1225 but the present buildings arise from the eighteenth and nineteenth centuries. An attractive bell tower guards the entrance and inside is a well kept small garden. The oblong church has a high painted ceiling and contains a rich array of silver ikons, chandeliers and incense burners. Many of the church artefacts are kept in the small museum which also houses the bones of a sea monster killed by French sailors off the coast here in 1860. There is a pleasant terrace café opposite the entrance to the monastery and good views from the headland down along the rocky shoreline.

BELLA VISTA ON FOOT

Nothing beats the spectacular views enjoyed from Bella Vista which is perched high in the mountains above the resort. Next to Mouse Island, it is the most photographed view on Corfu. There is a route by road which involves walking uphill in the direction of Corfu town for around 3km (2 miles) and taking the Lakones road and following this through all its uphill winds and twists for a further 6km (4 miles). By far the shorter and more interesting route is the old donkey trail.

Start walking back from the main beach and turn shortly opposite the taverna Calm. Stay right as the road forks a minute later and start to climb along this concrete road which soon reverts to track. About six or seven minutes later, just as this track reaches a summit and before it descends, take the wide path which leads off left. Some signs for Bella Vista are starting to appear along the route. Keep straight up to join a lovely old cobbled route. This leads steadily uphill through olive groves and woodlands finding an easier ascent than can ever be imagined, but it is still uphill! After around 30 minutes, or longer if it is very hot, Lakones is approached. On entering, turn left at the T junction to join the main road through the village. Make a mental note of this turn and the entry point on the main road for the return journey, if the intention is to return this way but there is an alternative. Follow left for Bella Vista and the spectacular views down over Paleokastritsa. There are cafés and tavernas on hand for refreshments. Some of the tavernas up here are expensive, like the Golden Fox, but for a good meal at a reasonable price, and an even better viewpoint, is the Castelino perched high up on the inland side of the road.

Those with time in hand may wish to continue walking along the road to the next village, Makrades, which has tavernas and tourist shops including roadside sellers offering home made wine, honey and herbs. It is a fairly easy, gentle uphill walk.

To return from Bella Vista by an

alternative route, also on country trails, set off back down the main road to a row of tourist shops on the right. Descend the concrete steps alongside which lead into an old trail. Bear right and keep following the trail which reverts to path in parts until a T junction is reached and turn left. Continue to follow the old path to reach a track (house amongst the trees on right) and turn left again. The track soon runs into surfaced road which leads back into Paleokastritsa.

A Day Up Mount Pandokrator (Pantocrator)

Pandokrator rises to 906mm (2,972ft) and is the highest mountain on the island. Although the top is scarred with masts, it has a monastery, and enough mountain atmosphere to make it an interesting visit. This excursion is by car and foot but the car does most of the uphill work and the walk is only along the final section of track on gently rising ground, except for the final short haul. About 45 minutes on foot is required for the final section or longer if the rich array of wild flowers to be found up there causes a serious distraction. Temperatures are lower up the mountain so keep a jumper handy, especially before May and, if it is very hot, carry some water. Sensible footwear is essential to cope with the stony track.

The points of interest include: the drive into the mountains; Strinilas

village; a walk to the mountain top; interesting wild flowers; Ano Korakiana and the display of sculptures.

The village to aim for to start the walk is Strinilas. This is reached from Corfu town by taking the coastal road north following signs to Ipsos and Kassiopi. Once Ipsos is reached, watch for the left turn at the end of the bay up to Spartilas and be prepared for a few tight bends. Beyond Spartilas look for the right turn to Strinilas. Most maps indicate an unmetalled road for the rest of the journey but the road is actually surfaced and generally good.

Strinilas is only a small village but has received an injection of new life with improved access. Even car parks have appeared and there are a couple of good tavernas in the small, shady platea. Both offer food at reasonable prices and do not forget to try the home made wine. The village square makes an interesting coffee stop on the way up and a useful lunch break on the way back, although picnickers will have little trouble finding a lunch spot along the route of the walk.

To reach the start, continue by car through the village and keep right where the road forks left to Petalia which can be seen close by. Keep on the road until the surface and the way ahead is track. Find a wide spot and park. Four-wheeled drive cars can be driven the rest of the way but the road is rough and, bearing in mind that the driver is responsible for damage to the underside, it is not advisable to take an ordinary hire car any further.

Odysseus on Corfu

Homer's Odyssey can arguably be described as the world's first novel complete with characters and a plot. Homer was actually a poet and a teller of myths and legends and his epic works, the *Iliad* and *Odyssey,* have become part of the literary heritage not just of Greece but of all nations of the world. The books represent two aspects of the Trojan War, an event which took place in the Mycenaean period which came to an abrupt end in 1200BC. The date of Homers work is not clearly known but thought to be around 700BC so he was relating legends which had been around for some 500 years. His works, a marriage of fact and fiction, have provided a battleground for scholars over centuries endeavouring to sort one from the other and identify fictional places with real locations.

The *Iliad* describes events in the east of the region, in what is now Turkey, but the *Odyssey* follows the travels of hero Odysseus, King of Ithaka, back home from the wars. Ithaka is one of the Ionian islands lying close to Kefalonia so scholars have endeavoured to identify mythical names with other locations in the Ionian islands which has generated many claims and counter claims from the islands themselves, and they are still arguing.

Apart from our hero Odysseus (Ulysses to the Romans), the story also has a 'goody' in the form of Athena, goddess of wisdom, who carefully guides Odysseus along his precarious voyage home, and a 'baddy', Poseidon, god of the sea.

Poseidon is so enraged with Odysseus that he sows nothing but disaster and torment in his path back towards his homeland and faithful wife who spends all of her time fending off a plague of would-be suitors.

Shipwrecked, exhausted and naked, Odysseus was washed ashore on the island of Scherie occupied by the peaceful Phaeacians. The mythical Phaeacians were peaceful and prosperous people, quiet and beloved by the gods, who lived on the mainland but were constantly troubled by their neighbours, the Cyclopes. They moved to set up home on an island at the end of the world, Scherie, to live in peace. Scherie, it is claimed, is an ancient name for Corfu and it is here where Odysseus was washed up. To finish this little episode, Athena visited the dreams of Princess Nausicaa, daughter of King Alkinoos, and, using the voice of Nausicaa's bosom friend, chastised her for not washing her beautiful clothes that she would soon need for her wedding. Next day, sure enough, Nausicaa went down to the sea with her friends to do some washing and, in a ball game afterwards, Athena directed the ball so it fell in the direction of Odysseus which then led to his discovery.

Popular belief on Corfu identifies Ermones as the beach where Odysseus was washed ashore. From here he was taken to the palace of Alkinoos (where the monastery now lies on the headland at Paleokastritsa?) and greeted as a god. Odysseus explained he was merely a castaway on his way home to Ithaka without revealing who he was. A ship was laid on the next day to take him home and it was that ship which Poseidon, in his anger, turned to stone. The rock representing the petrified ship is identified with a number of rocks around Corfu, including Mouse Island but particularly the one off Paleokastritsa.

Perhaps one rosy fingered dawn when gazing out onto a wine dark sea, the rock off Paleokastritsa might just turn into a ship and the monastery on the hill into a palace, who knows.

The rest now is on foot and it takes 45 minutes along this stony track to reach the summit but there is some interesting scenery and a whole gamut of wild flowers along the way. In April and May there are plenty of wild orchids to be found here including the man orchid, *Aceras anthropophorum,* the toothed orchid, *Orchis tridentata,* the beautiful yellow *Orchis provincialis* and the dainty *Orchis quadripunctata,* so called because of the four spots on the lip of the flower.

A solitary priest seems to be in charge of the monastery which is unspectacular, apart from its position. If he is around it may be possible to gain entry to the church to see the frescos otherwise it is kept locked. The present nineteenth-century building occupies the site of an earlier monastery built in 1347 which was destroyed in 1689. If it all seems peaceful and deserted, try the first week in August when celebrations are in hand to commemorate the saints name day. It was once a major celebration attracting people from all over the island and many slept in the cells by the church. It is not quite as big now but it still attracts the faithful. It is a great place to stop to catch breath and absorb the views which, on a good day, embrace not just the island itself but include Paxos and Kefalonia to the south and Albania to the east.

Retreat to the car on foot the same way. For a different route back to Corfu town, and for a look at one of the most incredible roads on the island for S-bends, return through Strinilas to the first junction and turn right to Sgourades. Beyond Sgourades look for a minor road left to Zigos. Although minor it is surfaced and good to drive apart from the occasional pot-hole. Turn left after Zigos to Sokraki and fork left on reaching Sokraki and left again on leaving this village. From here the road enters a seemingly endless and quite spectacular zig-zag down the mountainside offering, for those who dare take their eyes off the road, some fantastic views. Although the road is narrow, it is well surfaced and walled in parts.

Turn right on meeting the main road to head into Ano Korakiana. Keep an eye open on the left, at balcony level, as the village is entered to spot the sculptures of the Corfiot Arestides Zach Metallinos. Looking at the display of work on the balcony and again in the dusty workshop by the house, he seemed totally obsessed with sex and the female form.

The road from Korakiana leads down to join the main Paleokastritsa-Corfu road and a left turn here quickly leads back to town.

Car Tour 1.
Around The Skirts Of Pandokrator

This excursion out of Corfu town visits many resorts in the north-east corner of the island and is loaded with spectacular mountain scenery. Some of the island's busiest resorts are included in the tour as well as some of the quieter ones. The itinerary includes Gouvia, Dassia, Ipsos, Pyrgi, Barbati, Nissaki, Kalami, Kouloura and Kassiopi, returning inland via Episkepsis. Although it involves only 85km (53miles) of driving, there are more than enough highlights along the way to ensure that it consumes a full day. Be sure to pack a bathing costume too.

Leave Corfu town to the north following Paleokastritsa signs initially. The road joins the coast before Kondokali (Kontokali) is reached and looking out to sea here gives a view of **Lazeretto Island**. It is only a little island but what a history. During Venetian times it was a place of quarantine for ships carrying the plague and later it was a leper colony. Much more recently it was used as a place of execution for the communists in the civil war. For the very curious there are boat trips out to it from Corfu town.

Gouvia is the first stop along the way so turn off right at Kondokali to enter by the old coast road. This resort is not one of those places where the layout can be instantly appreciated. Although there is an attractive backdrop of mountains, the centre of the resort and the beach seem almost unrelated. The centre is strung along this approach road which is a few hundred yards inland from the beach so another right turn is required to head down to the sea front. At the southern end of Gouvia Bay lies a marina which will be finished one day, maybe! Remnants of an arched structure just on the northern side are the remains of the old

Venetian boatyards and a little further north is the attractively set shingle bay which is the town beach where sunbathers bathe and the active whizz around on water skis or hang from parachutes. But this is where it all happens.

Continue to head north and turn right following signs to Kassiopi where the main road swings left to cross the island to Paleokastritsa.

Dassia lies just a few kilometres further north. Although larger and busier, Dassia is similar in character to Gouvia. Shops and tavernas are strung out along the main road which lies several hundred yards inland from the coast. Some of the space between the main road and the beach is occupied by large hotels. Quietly located away from the road, the largely shingle beach is not very deep but it has plenty of length and is attractively set with views over to Albania. It is punctuated here and there by wooden platforms used either for water sports, of which there is a full range, or for sun bathing. One or two large hotels open onto the beach providing attractive grassed areas and facilities which are available to the public. It is a major resort with plenty happening both day and night. Dassia is also the location of a large Club Mediterranee which lies on the wooded headland to the north.

Ipsos, the next stop along the coast road, lies in the next bay to the north. It is a puzzle how it ever developed into a resort, let alone a lively resort. The narrow, shingle beach lies immediately adjacent to

Above: The beach at Gouvia

Below: The Venetian boatyard ruins

Above: Dassia has a long, narrow sand/shingle beach

Below: Ipsos, where the main road runs adjacent to the beach

the busy main road and sunbathers have little choice but suffer the road noise and pollution while catching a tan. This apart, the setting is attractive with the wooded foothills of Pandokrator rising steeply to the north and the mountains of Albania seeming ever closer. Inland from the main road leads almost immediately into countryside dominated by olive trees. It makes an attractive setting for accommodation which is springing up here, some with swimming pools. All the facilities in terms of bars, tavernas and discos lie on the inland side of the main road. The beach offers water sports but no refreshment facilities. For these you must cross the road.

Pyrgi shares the northern end of the same bay and much of the same character, although maybe a little quieter. From here the road climbs onto the steep mountainside and away from the coast. Some attention is needed along here to spot the small roads which link down to the coastal resorts. The first of these is down to Barbati and the road is through the archway which announces Barbati Beach.

Barbati beach, with its white shingle beach contrasting sharply with the deep blue of the sea, is quite spectacular. Bathed in quiet with hardly a murmur even from the sea, there is not too much around apart from a couple of hotels and a few villas scattered around the tree clad slopes but there are water sports available in the main season. There is also a taverna at the sea front which makes a great lunch spot if the tim-

ing is right. For some inexplicable reason, there are water taxis to take people to Ipsos.

From here it is back to the main road to continue north. The next challenge is finding the minor road down to the next resort, Nissaki, and it is very easy to drive past it.

Scenic **Nissaki** is located in a tiny bay and exudes an idyllic ambience. It has a small shingle beach with a jetty and tavernas, one perched above the sea. This is the one to sit in and watch the lazy activities on the beach and the boats coming and going along the shoreline. Much of the accommodation is in the form of villas and apartments which are tucked away on the wooded hillside.

Continuing northwards again along the main road, there is still another test in store. This time it is finding the small road which leads down to Kalami and Kouloura.

Kalami is the southernmost and larger of these two resorts. The writings of Gerald Durell have put Kalami firmly on the map for this is the location of the white house where he lived as a child. Now it is a water front taverna and remains mostly a point of interest for passing boat trips. The resort itself nestles intimately at the foot of the wooded hills looking directly into a sheltered bay. Tavernas front onto the shingle beach where a wooden jetty lends the feel that this is somewhere really Greek. All the usual beach furnishings are available as are canoes and pedaloes. Completely without road noise, this is a really tranquil, away from it all resort which has all the necessary amenities on hand.

Kouloura, the neighbouring bay, is within easy walking distance and walking is not a bad idea for there is limited space for cars and turning around can be a problem. Kouloura is nothing more than a picturesque small natural fishing harbour with a taverna. At least one rich Italian has found his idyll and built a big, well guarded house.

No further problems in finding roads now, from here there is just more mountain scenery to enjoy as the road winds its way to Kassiopi.

Kassiopi, one of the island's major resorts, is beautifully set below the now gentler slopes of Pandokrator. It was a fishing village long before the advent of tourism and the jewel in its crown is the spacious harbour from where the fishing fleet still operate as they have always done. It has a long history and there was a period in which it was more important than Corfu town. It was founded by settlers from Corinth in 360BC and became important under the Romans when it was visited by a number of notables which included Mark Antony and the Emperor Nero. At that time it minted its own coins and had its own temples. In the Venetian period it was an important outpost controlling the trade route down the channel between the island and Albania, hence the castle whose ruins can still be seen on the hillside above town.

Just about every kind of tourist shop can be found on the main street down to the harbour. Lace and cro-chet work are specialities of the village and this is the best place on the island to buy them. A spacious square abuts the harbour which easily accommodates the daily flood of tour buses without distracting too much from the atmosphere. Kassiopi is also the destination of boat trips from Corfu town and other nearby resorts. With the daily influx of day trippers, the town gets rather crowded in main season but it quietens down by 4pm and the residents then enjoy a more peaceful few hours. The town has spread well outside its original boundaries and has grown more touristy but not yet over commercialised. Much of the accommodation is provided by villas and apartments.

On the western side of the harbour stands the church of Our Lady of Kassiopi which is built on the site of one of the ancient temples from the Roman era. It was for a long time regarded as one of the most important shrines on the island and associated with several miracles.

Swimmers and sunbathers are not too well placed with only limited facilities. Small pebble coves just outside the town and flat rocks have to serve and in this respect the resort is not especially good for children. Water sports too are a bit restricted by the winds which often blow down the channel.

The route back from Kassiopi continues anticlockwise around the skirts of Pandokrator but there is one more resort in store yet, that of **Ag Spiridon**. Around 6km (4 miles) beyond Kassiopi a sign for the beach of

Above: Barbati with its spectacular white shingle beach

Below: Kouloura should not be missed, but parking can be a problem

St Spiridon indicates a right turn. This leads down to a small sandy beach which is usually quiet but is a favourite spot for the Corfiots themselves so tends to be busier at weekends. At the moment there is just one taverna but there is some building now in progress. At the western end is the Andinioti lagoon which is favoured by bird watchers and by duck shooters in autumn. A bridge leads across the channel and from here there are broad tracks which lead to Cape Ag Ekaterinis.

Continuing along the north coast look for the left turn signposted Episkepsis. This is the route back and if there is time left in the day, a brief stop at the latter village offers a chance to see some of the old Venetian houses. A further 14km (9 miles) and the road, after passing through Spartilas, rejoins the outward route at Pyrgi. From here it does not take too long to reach Corfu town.

CAR TOUR 2. THE NORTH WEST FRONTIER

This tour of the north-west corner of the island is spiced with yet more mountainous scenery, one of Corfu's most picturesque resorts in Paleokastritsa, fascinating villages, a castle and miles of sandy beaches. Starting from Corfu town the itinerary includes Paleokastritsa, Lakones, Makrades, Krini for Angelokastro, the Trumbeta pass, Ag Georgiou, Ag Stefanos, Sidari, Roda and back to Corfu town via the agricultural villages of Platonas and Episkopi then the Trumbeta pass again. About 120km (75miles) of driving is involved and there is plenty to see so set aside a whole day, preferably with an early start. Pack a bathing costume, there are plenty of good beaches, and for those planning a picnic there is nowhere more romantic than Angelokastro. There is plenty of opportunity for diners although Paleokastritsa is best avoided as it gets busy and is one of the most expensive resorts on the island.

A fast road leads north out of Corfu town all the way to Paleokastritsa and, with normal traffic conditions, the journey takes around 30mins. Paleokastritsa is featured as a day out (see page 60) and the resort is described in some detail there. Head back along the road to Corfu town for around 3km (2 miles) and turn left to Lakones. The road winds and twists appreciably as it leads up the mountainside to the village itself which is strung out along the roadside. Do not be tempted to stop the car yet to admire the views or waste your film, they get much better very shortly. The place to stop for truly breathtaking views down over Paleokastritsa is in the region of the café/restaurant Bella Vista. If it is time for lunch, the Golden Fox is well situated but very expensive and equally good food is found at Castelino which is perched high up on the inland side of the road and the view is quite stunning.

Preceding page: Kassiopi harbour. There is a small pebbly beach here

The road climbs less steeply to **Makrades**, the next village and, by keeping an eye over to the left, it is possible to catch a sight of the castle of Angelokastro sat firmly astride a craggy tower of rock. Two tavernas, Colombos and Mimoza, await at the entrance to Makrades which are good but be warned, they are popular with the coach tours and get crowded at lunch times. Tourist shops have sprung up to take advantage of this regular trade and for a small village, it is surprisingly commercial. Lots of the villagers join in with their own wayside stalls selling home made wine, honey and herbs. Once through the forest of waving arms trying to persuade passing motorists to stop, turn left to Krini and follow signs now to Angelokastro. Only a short time ago it was necessary to park at Krini and proceed on foot but now the road leads right to the foot of the castle. There is some leg work left, about 10 minutes climbing up the steep, stony path.

Angelokastro was built by the Epirot Michael I Angelos in the thirteenth century. It was he who seized Corfu from the Venetians in 1214 following the collapse of Byzantium and kept a grip on the island for the next 44 years. The strategic location of the castle is best appreciated from the top where Corfu town is easily visible. This clear line of communication enabled the local garrison to signal the approach of enemy vessels back to the island's major stronghold, the old fort. Angelokastro was called into action to resist the Turks but has the proud record of never falling in battle. Inside the castle, to the left, there is the small chapel of Ag Kiriaki to find. It is in a cave under the rocks with steps leading down to it. Some remnants of frescos still exist there including one of the Virgin and Child behind the altar and a smaller fresco to the left. Perched on the higher ground is the small white chapel of the Archangels Michael and Gabriel, normally unlocked, and in front of it are a number of rock-cut tombs. It is a wonderful viewpoint too and Paleokastritsa can be seen with all its bays, headlands and convolutions.

Return through Krini to Makrades and turn left to continue through Vistonas. Dramatic views open up as the road climbs to still higher levels, higher even than Trumbeta pass which is reached shortly. Turn left on joining the Trumbeta road ignoring shortly the turn off for Roda and continue along the Sidari road for the moment. The route chosen for the next destination, Ag Georgiou is not the most direct but it avoids the bus and coach route and traverses attractive countryside. Some 5km (3 miles) after the Roda junction, on reaching Agros, turn left following signs to Dafni. The sheer verdancy of the island is overwhelming in these country areas as here where the road winds through olive groves which crowd close to the road. But for Hotel Bella Vista, Dafni would probably pass

Following page: The castle at Angelokastro

Above: The beautiful beach at Ag. Georgiou (north)

Below: Sidari, the general view of the coast, west of the town

unnoticed. Turn left to Arilas soon after then follow signs to Ag Georgiou. Good views open up on descending into the bay to reveal the magnificent setting of this resort. On arriving above the bay, ignore the road which loops off left, this is a dead end, and take the one ahead which descends steeply.

Ag Georgiou is higgledy-piggledy as a resort but attractive nevertheless. Poised between two headlands, it has all the necessary ingredients, a beautiful beach, hotels, tavernas, shops but all suitably disorganised and without even a proper road system to connect them. Its long, golden sandy beach is superb and there are tavernas enough opening directly on to it. All the usual beach furniture, sun beds and umbrellas are there for hire and there is a fair selection of water sports for the active including pedaloes for those taking things a little easier. Driving the length of the resort is not so straight forward but it can be done with a tiny stretch through sand. Rough seas are more common on this side of the island which the surfers appreciate, this apart, it is good for families. It is a quiet resort, fairly isolated with just two buses a day to Corfu town. Visiting anywhere else could be a problem without transport. Fortunately, the resort is self sufficient.

Head back to follow signs to Arilas then continue down to the coast for a look at one of the island's newest resorts, Arilas Bay.

Arilas Bay has a long stretch of good sand but without too much depth. The road directly behind is no problem since it carries little or no traffic. There are plenty of tavernas, cafés and shops with a lot of them on the approach road. Some of the accommodation is just inland as is the small village where there are rooms to let. Not as attractive as Ag Georgiou but much more accessible by car. Expect nothing more than a quiet resort. All this area is now opening up to tourism and it is only a short step along the road north to the next emerging resort, Ag Stef-anos.

Ag Stefanos is pleasantly set in a crescent shaped bay. It has a good sandy beach which has some depth in the centre. All the usual facilities are on hand, beach furniture, water sports and tavernas. As yet it is a small low-key resort with development taking place inland from the beach and overall it is ordinary rather than attractive.

It is a fairly easy run into Sidari from here along the hillside passing through the sprawling village of Avliotes.

Sidari has plenty of buzz and has quickly grown into one of the island's major resorts. Its main attraction is a long, long stretch of fine sand which shelves only gently into the water making it ideal for children. Just about every facility imaginable is available on the beach and it may not even be necessary to stir from a sun lounger, apart from waving an arm, for an ice cream or a drink. The sea is less rough along this coast which makes it ideal for the ever popular canoes and pedaloes but they are not the only water sports by any means. Boat hire too is popular and there are plenty on offer. The main road runs marginally inland alongside the beach and is lined with tourist shops of every description and buying a chocolate croissant or changing money offers no problems. A one-way system operates for traffic.

At the extreme western edge of the resort the long straight beach is replaced by rocky coves. Winter gales and storms over the centuries have cut and sculpted the soft rocks around these bays into interesting shapes and none more so than the rocks known as **Canal d'Amour**. This was once an arch formed by the rocks and the legend was that anyone swimming through the channel while it was in the shade would win their hearts desire. Unfortunately, the elements are quite relentless and unaware of local tradition. Further erosion has seen the roof of the arch collapse but the legend lives on, at least in the old postcards still sold. Mother nature is not the only sculptor in these parts, man has lent a hand too by cutting terraces out of the rocky headlands to take rows of sun loungers.

There is a new road which leads over to Roda, the final port of call on this tour. Head back first along the Corfu road but prepare to turn left into the new section which has not yet made it onto maps. Turn left on entering for the sea front and parking.

Roda's transformation from a simple fishing village to a modern resort is all but complete, although no doubt it will continue to expand. Its long beach is made up of a series of small bays with breakers at intervals. It is sandy in the main with a fair depth to the beach but seaweed is a problem in parts. Good level access to the beach and shallow seas make it ideal for families. There are plenty of tourist facilities on hand in shops, tavernas and bars which stretch out along the approach roads with some along the shore. Although its setting is unspectacular, the older part adds some character and with the hills a little further away, pedal cycles are popular as is horse riding.

Acharavi together with Ag Stefanos lie almost next door to Roda and share the same bay. The beach is a mix of sand and shingle which shelves only gently into the sea and is good for children. All the usual beach facilities are on hand and there is plenty of opportunity for water sports. It is a modern, developing resort where shops line the main road which runs inland and parallel to the beach but, like so many resorts and villages on the island, it lacks a focal point.

In returning to Corfu from Roda, choices are possible. The coastal route via Kassiopi is slow but scenic, the route via Episkepsis is included in tour 1 so recommended here, and the easiest driving, is back directly to Trumbeta.

The Olive

Introduced into Corfu on a large scale by the Venetians, the olive is ideally suited to the island's climate. Estimates on the current population are usually put at 3 to 4 million trees.

Known from Crete as early as 3500BC, the olive has been central to the existence of the Mediterranean peoples for millennia. Although grown primarily for oil for cooking, the oil is also used as a lubricant, for lighting, soap making and in ointments and liniments for the skin. The fruit itself, the olive, is also eaten but Corfu's olives are exclusively used for oil production.

The tree is evergreen with leathery lance-shaped leaves which are dark green above and silvery beneath. With age the trunks become gnarled and twisted adding considerably to the character of the tree. It takes 4 to 8 years for a tree to start bearing fruit but full production is not reached until after 15 to 20 years and it may then continue for centuries with proper care. The tree is erratic in that not every year produces a good crop, unless a suitable regime of irrigation and feeding is rigorously followed, but more often good crops are expected every other year. Whitish flowers borne in loose clusters arrive in late spring which rely on the wind for pollination. The fruit which follows takes 6 to 8 months to reach full maturity for only then does it give the maximum yield of oil. This means that harvesting takes place throughout the winter months, from December through until March, the perfect complement to working in the tourist season. Fruits for eating are collected before maturity and need special treatment with dilute caustic lye and salt to kill the extreme bitterness. There are hundreds of named varieties of olives, both for oil and for eating, which are propagated from hard wood cuttings or from leaf cuttings under mist propagation. Few of these varieties can actually be seen on the island for the variety introduced by the Venetians is still used almost exclusively.

Olive oil is produced in a selection of grades, the very finest oil from the first pressing is known as virgin oil and this is the grade preferred for salad dressing. It is a good buy to take home too and can be found on the supermarket shelves in 5 litre containers. The second grade of oil is the pure, a blend of virgin oil and refined oil, which is the third grade. Refined oil is made from the lampante grade, so called because it is used for lamp fuel, by treatment to remove the acid, the colour and the odour. Lampante is obtained from a second pressing of the residual pulp.

The wood too is of great value. It is very hard, strongly grained and takes a fine polish, ideal for carving, cabinet work and toys. Olive wood carving is very popular on the island and there are a number of shops exclusively selling this type of work. It is also used as a slow burning fuel and for making charcoal for which the Greeks have a great demand.

Botanically, the olive, (*Olea europea*), belongs to the Oleaceae family and has some interesting and familiar relatives like ash, privet, jasmine and lilac.

A venerable olive tree shades an old olive crushing stone at Tebloni

CAR TOUR 3.
MID-WEST VILLAGES

The villages visited on this tour lie in the lee of the high ground behind the western shore. An insurance against the roving eye of marauders who regularly plied the coast in search of bounty. Many were probably established in the sixteenth century when Corfu received an influx of immigrants from the Peloponnese and Crete. The tour covers around 85km (53miles) of driving and includes Doukades, Liapades, Ropa Plain, Danilia Village, Gianades, Ermones, Pelekas, Glifada, Sinarades, Ag Gordis, Kinopiastes and the Achilleion Palace en route back to Corfu Town. Go prepared for swimming but exercise caution should the sea be rough, taking note of warning flags where they operate.

Follow the road out of Corfu Town to Paleokastritsa as far as Gouvia.

Danilia Village lies about 2km inland from Gouvia and is signposted. See opening times below before making a detour. Part of the complex used to be an open-air cinema, located further along the road towards Ropa Plain, but this has fallen into disuse. All that remains is a large mangled metal structure, which was the screen, and shuttered pay box. Modelled on the style of a typical Corfiot village, Danilia enjoys a peaceful rural location. It was built by a local family and opened in 1977. A range of traditional craftwork is sold in the shops lining the

village street and an excellent folk museum is worth a visit for itself alone. The museum's collection of 🛖 artefacts fills several rooms and depicts Corfiot life down the centuries. In the village square stands the bell 🛖 tower and church of Ag Irene along with the obligatory kafenion. Evenings are the time when the village really comes to life. Danilia is the venue for fun and entertainment on a grand scale when coachloads of people roll up for dinner with free wine and a Greek floor show. Although most people arrive by coach, there is nothing to stop individuals from turning up and paying the fixed entry price at the door. Opening times are limited in the morning and do not always fit easily into a touring itinerary. Open: Monday to Saturday 10am-1pm and 6-10pm; closed Sunday. ☎ (0661) 91621, 90151.

At **Tsavros**, the main road heads to cross the island. Lining the road along here are some larger commercial enterprises selling olive wood and leather products. An unusual ✳ encounter on a Greek island is a factory producing fine bone china. As might be guessed, it has connections with a 'Potteries' town in England and is open to the public. A little further along is the **Ameco Distill-** ✳ **ery**, the Kumquat Liqueur Factory and Exhibition Centre. Visitors can drop in and taste before buying from the wide range of products on display. Kumquats originate in China and Japan and were brought to Corfu early in the twentieth century by an Englishman, Merlin. He grew them in Dassia, at a place now called Merlin, but the north of the island provides the best climate. Today, kumquats are grown in the vicinity of Platonas, Nimfes and Acharavi and harvested between January and the end of March. The best and most natural product, with a colour to match, is made with the juice whilst the orange colour derives from distillation of the skin. Besides kumquat orientated tipples, the company produces a whole range of drinks from a selection of liqueurs, spirits and wine, including brandy. Open from March to October; Monday to Saturday 9am-6pm; closed Sunday.

The right turn up to Doukades is easily missed. Keep a sharp look out for the turn off as the road narrows and starts to wind and twist down to Paleokastritsa. **Doukades** still retains a sleepy air, most tourists intent on weaving their way through and on. That is unless larger than life Elizabeth, from the taverna of the same name, does not manage to entice you to linger a while at one of her tables. She is well known for her good food but is quite happy to serve a coffee or ouzo. An evening meal here, with a bottle of Elizabeth's husband's full-bodied red wine, watching the comings and goings of the local population is an absorbing experience. Park at the entrance to the village and explore on foot. A lively 'panayiros' to St John, around the 25 June is held annually with over thirty lambs roasted simultaneously on spits and music and dancing.

Return to the main road and turn left, then take the next right to Liapades. Cross the major road then meet a T-junction. Choices here are right, down to **Liapades Beach** by the Elli Beach Hotel or left to Liapades village. Park on the edge of the village and walk. The small sand/shingle beach has sunbeds and pedaloes but there is limited parking. A taverna overlooks the beach and another, the Cricketers, lies a little further up the road.

Liapades is quite a large hillside village where it is still possible to find vestiges of an old way of life. A Plane tree presides over the small platea with its cluster of kafeneons and dilapidated church. Old Venetian mansions among twisting alleyways tell a story of past elegance.

Follow the road south along the **Ropa Plain** for a couple of kilometres then turn right, into a narrow surfaced road for Gianades. The road wends along the edge of Ropa Plain to skim the low foothills behind the coast. During the Italian occupation of the early 1940s, Ropa Plain was drained to reclaim highly fertile agricultural ground. It is still intensively farmed to this day and is where a good concentration of little old ladies on donkeys can be found, although they do pop up anywhere. **Kanakades** has a small by-pass road off left which avoids the narrow road up through the village ahead. A Persian bead tree shades the tiny platea here, where the church keeps an eye

Following Page: Sidari, the Canal d'Amour, adjacent to a sandy beach

Above: The lamb roast at Doukades

Below: The verdant Ropa Plain

on ouzo sipping locals sitting outside the kafeneon/shop. Again the road narrows to pass through Marmaro before meeting a crossroads. Turn up right.

The sizeable village of **Gianades** perches higher up the hillside and provides a good viewing platform out over the Ropa Plain. Old houses with sun-bleached roofs, geraniums in painted tin cans, white steps and balconies denote a Greek way of life not yet glazed with too much tourism. Return back down to the crossroads and turn right, a further right at the T-junction leads to the beach.

Ermones has poor access from this side of the beach for those lacking some agility. The sand/shingle beach, with watersports facilities and tavernas, is enclosed by steep hillsides. A funicular, serving residents of the Ermones Beach hotel, makes an incongruous feature. Park on the roadside above the beach and walk down or approach from the far side via Vatos. A stream, the River Ermones, flows across the beach and is one of the sites reputedly connected with Homer's *Odyssey*. Legend states how Odysseus was found exhausted and naked here by the Phaeacian princess Nausicaa and her maidens. See box page 66.

Head inland and note the road ahead, as the main route swings right to cross a bridge, which leads to the **Corfu Golf and Country Club**. This enterprise shares the same owner as the Corfu Hilton. A wide range of facilities is offered at this championship course, which enjoys a green and tranquil setting on the Ropa Plain. The English run Ropa Valley Riding Stables also operates from the golf club site. A further road down to Ermones beach goes off right just after crossing the bridge. **Vatos** is the small tranquil village now off right in the shelter of Ag Georgios hill. Keep right at the main fork. This pretty road leads through olive groves towards Pelekas. A sign off right, along a concrete track, indicates the monastery of Mirtiotissa (Our Lady of the Myrtles) but the route is rough and steep, shortly becoming unsuitable for vehicles. Located in a setting of golden sand and steep cliffs, the small white monastery holds court over this once remote beach which becomes crowded with boat trippers during the tourist season.

Glifada Beach is more easily accessible, as burgeoning development testifies. Follow signs to Glifada right and wind down past the Glifada Beach Hotel to a large car park. The long, deep stretch of golden sand is enclosed by steep vegetation covered hillsides. Here, in this very picturesque setting, there is no shortage of beach and watersports facilities. Head back uphill and continue rising through olive grove to Pelekas.

Pelekas wraps itself around the hilltop, its popularity evident in the tourist trappings and new building which tend to mask the character of the village. Above the village is a panoramic viewpoint, with telescope, known as the 'Kaiser's Throne'. A name which has stuck from the days when Kaiser Wilhelm II motored from the Achilleion Palace to watch the summer sunset. The wide ranging views over the island are magnificent. Continue on through Pelekas to descend the far side of the hill. On the first hairpin bend below the village, a signposted track leads off right to Pelekas beach. This route is not recommended except for four-wheeled drive vehicles and walkers, better to opt for the surfaced road a little further south. Go right on meeting the crossroads for Sinarades and keep an eye open in around 3km for a sign to the Yaliskari Palace Hotel. A diversion right here leads steeply down the wooded hillside to Pelekas beach. The surfaced road ends just above the beautiful sandy beach where development is still very low key. Shortly before reaching Sinarades, the village of **Koumarades** lies up to the left. This traditional backwater is unaffected by tourism and has an intriguing number of wells in the centre.

Sinarades is reached after keeping right, where the road forks left to Corfu Town. This is another fairly large village best explored on foot. Cafés and shops front the central square where there is parking. Worth a visit and the main attraction is the Folkloric Museum of Central Corfu, a typical nineteenth-century village house with contents. Usually open from 9.30am-2.30pm. Find it by taking the narrow signposted road opposite the campanile tower, further along the main road past the centre. Follow through Sinarades

and turn right to head swiftly down to the fast developing resort of Ag Gordis.

The appeal of **Ag Gordis** lies in a magnificent backdrop of steeply wooded hills and long expanse of mainly sandy beach. Park on the outskirts in season as no concession has been made for cars to park near the beach. This is a very self-contained resort with no shortage of tourist shops and facilities including a wide variety of watersports. A wooden walkway connects tavernas and café/bars behind the beach. Leave Ag Gordis by the same road or take the narrow more scenic but circuitous route up through Kato Garouna before swinging left to head north back to Corfu. Pass close to the hill village of **Kinopiastes**, whose famed Tripa Taverna serves delicious 'mezedes' and attracts coachloads of visitors for traditional evenings of music and dancing, accompanied by copious quantities of food and drink at a set price. Once through Milia, watch for a right turn to Gastouri and the Achilleion Palace, a further 2km up this road.

The **Achilleion Palace** was the dream home of the tragic Empress Elizabeth of Austria. A culmination of her long-standing love affair with Corfu and enthusiasm for Greek mythology and literature. Elizabeth requested a palace 'worthy of Achilles' after whom it was named and, naturally, Achilles figures strongly in the décor. Unfortunately, the Italian architects applied Victorian ideals of ornate garishness to the design which has attracted adverse com-

Above: Pelekas village

Below: Glifada, a good sandy beach with tavernas

Above and below: Two views of the Achilleion Palace, the dream home of Empress Elizabeth of Austria. The neglected statues in the garden were cleaned ahead of a European Union meeting.

ment ever since. Built in the early 1890s, Elizabeth's enjoyment of her summer palace was abruptly ended in 1898, when she was assassinated. Kaiser Wilhelm II later bought and used the palace until 1914 when it reverted to use as a military hospital during World War I. It then came into the hands of the Greek Government and was converted into a casino in 1962, which is now based at the Corfu Hilton. A clutter of tourist paraphernalia announces the palace entrance and parking is along the roadside. Only the ground floor, with public WCs, is open to the public. Memorabilia belonging to both Elizabeth and the Kaiser are on display in the rooms directly off the large entrance hall. A talking point here is the odd saddle-seat used by the Kaiser at his writing desk. An impressive bronze of the wounded Achilles dominates the statuary in the interesting gardens and their elevated position provides wonderful panoramic views.

The quickest way back to Corfu Town is to return back to the Sinarades-Corfu road and turn right.

CAR TOUR 4. SOUTHERN HILLS AND HOLLOWS

Long established resorts, such as Benitses, Messongi and Kavos, and new discoveries like Mora'itika and Ag Georgios are the package on offer in this tour. The hills behind the coastal road, as far as Messongi, hide a delightful rural road used on the return which contrast sharply with the remote appeal of the southern tip. If swimming is on the agenda treat choppy seas with caution.

Head out of Corfu Town following signs to the airport and Lefkimmi. A few kilometres past the airport keep left at Vrioni to follow the main coastal road south. This road is quite narrow for the volume of traffic, squeezed up against the shore as it is by a range of hills. Perama is passed in a flash with nowhere to park and is probably best visited on foot via the causeway from Kanoni. The piers of the 'Kaiser's Bridge' stand forlornly by the roadside their connecting arch removed to allow traffic through. It once connected the jetty for the 'royal yacht' with the grounds of the Achilleion Palace above.

Benitses is soon reached. Despite the mass exodus of many of the young set to Kavos, Benitses still swings at night. It has little to commend it as a beach resort although a range of watersports is available. Tourist requirements are well catered for but the constant traffic and limited pavements exclude it as a family resort. The nucleus of the old fishing village it once was is worth a look and maybe be surprised at how close it lies to verdant countryside. A Roman villa once stood close behind the village but all that is left are some walls of its bath-house. Tiny shingle beaches near Strongili are more an attempt to make something out of nothing.

Mora'i'tika is a growing resort, having long overtaken neighbouring Messongi. Most facilities ribbon the main road, which at this point starts to move inland away from the shore. The remains of a Roman villa and bath house have been discovered nearby. Many apartments lie between the road and the sea which keeps the mainly sand, with some shingle, beach free of traffic. Restaurants and cafés abut the beach where sunbeds and watersports are available. A good beach and mix of quiet and lively make this a suitable resort for families. A small river separates Mora'i'tika from Messongi, which is reached by keeping ahead to cross a small bridge, as the main road goes inland to the right, then turning left. This narrow road skirts behind Messongi and on along the coast to the fishing village of Boukari.

Set back off the main road, **Messongi** has an enigmatic quality with the trappings of a resort but the air of a quiet backwater. The beach is narrow and similar in texture to that of Mora'i'tika. Despite surrounding hotels, the village has still managed to retain a separate identity with a number of small shops and beachside tavernas. Return to the main road and continue left through Ano (upper) Messongi. The road now traverses the middle of the island's tail which, although flatter, is very green and cloaked with an abundance of olive groves. If time allows, side trips off left lead through interesting villages to remote beaches. Signposted to the right, is the developing resort of Ag Georgios (south), close to Lake Korission.

Ag Georgios (south) is 3km (2 miles) from the main road, which

makes it fairly isolated away from the main season. It is the usual haphazard straggle of most Corfiot resorts, a ribbon of accommodation and facilities along the roadside. Cycling is a good means of getting around the flatter terrain at the tip of the island. Two good sand beaches, separated by a short stretch of rocky coast and backed by low cliffs, offer sunbeds and various watersports but the superb sand bar, which encloses Lake Korission at the north end of the resort, has good access and is a popular spot. A good choice of resort for young families and those who like some quiet and isolation. Perhaps not so good for those who like to be out and about most of the time.

Back on the main road heading south, note the Venetian bell-tower of the monastery at **Argirades**. A right turn from Marathias leads to yet another developing resort with fine sandy beach, **San Barbara**. Not at all touristy, **Ano Lefkimmi**, **Lefkimmi** and **Potami** merge into one and are the hub of the agricultural community in the south. This is the main wine producing area on Corfu and a good place to observe real Corfiot life. A wobbly bailey bridge crosses the river at Potami which is invitingly overlooked by tavernas and cafés.

A couple of kilometres of piecemeal development, amongst trees lining the shore, announces the approach of **Kavos**. The village itself is another monument to lack of planning control. Streets too narrow for pedestrians and cars and a solid jum-

Above: Koumarades is still a quiet backwater where the tradtional life of Corfu survives

Below: The view of Parga as your ship reaches the harbour

ble of cheek by jowl bars. No shortage of tourist facilities here, especially for the young and lively. This is definitely decibel city, party all night and sleep on the beach all day which reaches its zenith in July and August. An attractive sandy beach and shallow sea stretch as far as the eye can see and face across to the mainland. The whole resort gets into gear early in the season with just about every facility and wide range of watersports available. A pleasant walk from Kavos follows a track to the southernmost tip of the island, Cape Asprokavos, and ruined Moni Panagia Arkoudillas. Allow two hours for the return trip.

From Kavos return north by the same route initially. Just after Ano Messongi, where the main road does a right turn, keep ahead for Strongili and Ag Deka. An optional side trip to Gardiki Castle occurs just before this point. Go left to Ag Matt-heos and turn left in around 3km (2miles) for Lake Korission. After a further fork left the thirteenth-century **Gardiki Castle** lies by the roadside on the right. Only the walls remain intact. Return to the main route which then winds up and along the hillside to return parallel with the outward coastal road down right. It leads through pleasant rural scenery and small hamlets to **Ag Deka**, where magnificent views open up over Corfu Town to the mainland. Negotiate hairpin bends on the descent and, on meeting the main road at Milia, turn right to return to Corfu Town.

EXCURSIONS FROM THE ISLAND

There are a number of excursions on offer from the island either by coach or boat. The two most popular destinations are Parga on the mainland and the nearby island of Paxos (Paxi) which may include Antipaxos (Antipaxi). Boat trips sometimes offer Parga alone or together with Paxos while coach trips to Parga usually include some of the ancient sites which lie in the region.

The Athens bus from Corfu, and there are three daily, usually stops at Parga and this is perhaps the most economical way to travel. Check details at the main tourist office in Corfu.

Weekly excursions are also available to Albania but these are tightly organised and need to be booked several days in advance to sort out the red tape, passport details etc. Apart from the cost of the trip there is also a visa charge on entry and this must be paid in a hard currency, sterling, dollars or marks. Overall the trip is expensive. The nature of the excursion varies but usually includes a visit to a local archaeological site while leaving time to visit one of two towns, Achisaranda or Eximilia, with free time to explore. It departs Corfu town at 9am and arrives back on Corfu at 7pm with the crossing taking around 90 minutes.

Preceding page: The river at Potami from the wobbly bailey bridge

1. Parga and the Ancient Sites

Mainland scenery is an added bonus to this tour which here describes all the nearby ancient sites, the Nekromantion, Kassope and the Monastery of Zalonga. All these sites may not necessarily be included and it is wise to check the precise itinerary with the tour operator before booking. Unless there is a party of four, the cost of ferrying the car over to the mainland tilts the economics in favour of the coach. If there is an option to travel by car, consider a one night stopover which, apart from July and August, should present no problems. Roads in this part of the mainland are good and fast and normally, with only light traffic, driving is comfortable. Parga has beautiful beaches so be sure to pack a bathing costume.

Passengers disembark from the coach for the ferry trip over to Igoumenitsa on the mainland which takes only 1 hour 15 minutes on one of the modern boats. Igoumenitsa itself is nothing more than a port and has little to offer so the coach loads up and sets off south immediately down to Parga. This 50km (31 miles) journey is usually accomplished in under the hour.

The old fishing village of **Parga** nestles intimately into the curve of a small bay adjacent to a Venetian castle sat atop a promontory. Set amidst olive groves against a mountain backdrop with a sprinkling of tiny white churches, sandy beaches and offshore islands, Parga is one of the most picturesque resorts in the whole of mainland Greece. It is one of the few places where Greek tourism possibly still exceeds international tourism but the balance is slowly changing. Development is small scale and away from the village so much of the old character is retained amongst its narrow streets and alleyways. It is not the sort of place to leave in a hurry but, like many places throughout Greece though, it can become very crowded during the peak holiday season.

The main harbour fairly bustles with throngs of people eating out at the numerous waterside tavernas or idly shopping and fishing boats and ferry boats coming and going. This is where the ferry arrives and departs for Corfu. Endless time can be spent wandering the narrow streets and alleyways all packed with tourist shops, mini-markets and eating places but beyond the promontory lies splendid **Valtos Beach**. To find it, walk up the village streets as though heading for the castle. At the highest point there is a choice, either to head up left to the castle or continue over to the beach. Valtos Beach offers a magnificent crescent of sand backed by pine and olive and is largely unspoilt. Sun beds and parasols are available for hire and there are some water sports but it is still mainly low key. It is a great beach for swimming.

Save time too for exploring the **Norman-Venetian castle** where the Lion of St Mark, the symbol of Venice can still be seen, testament to four hundred years of Venetian rule. De-

Above: The shopping area behind Parga's harbour

Below: The picturesque fishing village of Longos (Loggos) Paxos

fending Parga was important to the Venetians who regarded it as the eyes and ears of Corfu and at that time most of the inhabitants lived within the castle walls. But in that period Parga was almost constantly at war fighting off the Albanian Muslims. It was the people of Parga who supplied arms to the neighbouring Suliotes to help them resist the Turks. Ali Pasha with 6,000 of his fellow Albanians laid siege to Parga in 1800 but with Russia now on the political scene it was aborted. He tried again in 1807 but found an easier route in 1817 by buying it from the British. They had acquired it from the French who in turn had only enjoyed a brief period of rule. After four centuries of continuous fighting to preserve their freedom, the Parganiotes were dismayed at being sold to Ali Pasha and made a mass attempt, all 4,000 men, women and children, to leave the town and sail away but were prevented from doing so by the English.

The ruins are amazingly extensive and there is no charge to enter. Opening hours are from 8am to 8pm.

Many people are intrigued by the small white church high on the headland to the east and, if there is time to spare, it is easy enough to walk up to it although it is fairly steep in parts. It takes around 45 minutes to reach the top and the reward is an unrivalled panoramic view of the resort, although good views are obtained without neces-

sarily climbing the whole way. Good footwear is advisable.

Leave the quay at Parga by following the road out east. Keep round right to follow close to the shore where the exit road goes up left. Continue ahead to pass between hotels, rooms and tavernas and, in around 10 minutes, reach a large supermarket on the right. Turn right immediately afterwards onto a fenced-in path initially which soon leads steeply up through the olive groves. The path eventually runs into track and continues up. Take care not to miss the path up right to the church, partially hidden by olive trees, just before the track begins to descend over the hill.

The next destination, the **Nekromantion of Ephyra**, is just a little ᴨ further south in the region of Mesopotamia which now straddles the ancient site. All there is to see now lies just a few hundred yards uphill from this village.

The remains of the Sanctuary to Hades and Persephone are situated on a hill above the confluence of the rivers Kokytos and Acheron, a branch of the mythical River Styx. In ancient times the site was believed to be the entrance to the Underworld (Hades). The myth relating to this oracle tells how Hermes would bring the souls of the dead to the shores of Lake Aherousia where, on payment of an 'obolos' (farthing), Charon would row them across to Hades. The fourth century BC

Preceding page: Fruit seller on Kavos beach

Nekromantion was built over a much earlier settlement which followed the same cult. The Oracle of the Dead developed around a belief that the souls of the dead could tell the future of the living. Homer relates in his Odyssey how Odysseus himself visited the oracle to consult with the dead and this was a few centuries before the present sanctuary was constructed. Besides undergoing the usual purification rituals associated with oracular consultations, evidence also suggests the use of hallucinatory drugs. This supports the theory that petitioners were induced into a highly emotional state before being allowed into the shrine. Disorientation was further heightened as the unfortunate victim had to negotiate a dark labyrinth to reach the inner sanctum. Here, further chicanery was enacted with the use of a windlass (remains in the museum at Ioannina) which was in all probability used to embellish the charade by winding figures up from below.

At the entrance to the site is an excellent plan carved in stone which helps to identify the layout of the ruins. The remains are remarkable in that many walls are still intact. In an inner room, an iron ladder leads down through a hole in the floor to an underground room.

Ancient Kassope and the Monastery of Zalonga lies still further south and leaves another 40km (25miles) of driving. A left turn is required on meeting the Arta road and another left turn shortly afterwards following signs to Paramithia. Kassope now appears on the signposts along with the nearest village, Kamarina. On the way up to Kamarina keep an eye open ahead for an early view of the dramatic hilltop statue to the Suliot women.

Kassope, built on a south facing plateau in the fourth century BC on the site of an earlier Bronze Age settlement, became an important member of the Epirot League from 232 BC until it was destroyed by Roman troops in 167BC. Although it was rebuilt, it was finally abandoned in 31BC when Augustus decreed that the population should resettle at Nikopolis, near Preveza. It was a centre for the worship of Aphrodite and is among the best preserved ancient towns. The compact geometrically laid-out ruins, protected by a polygonal wall, were only discovered forty years ago. There is a useful plan by the entrance to show the layout of the old city.

The **Monastery of Zalonga**, a further half kilometre up the mountain, is the scene of a more recent drama when Suliots, a tribe of Christian Epirots, sought refuge there in 1802 from attack by Ali Pasha. High above the monastery is a memorial, in the form of a sculpture, to the women and children who escaped capture by flinging themselves over the precipice.

2. A CRUISE TO PAXOS AND ANTIPAXOS

Organised cruises leave mostly from Corfu town but also from Kavos in

Above: Monument to the Suliot women near Zalonga

Below: The harbour area at Gaios on Paxos

Sea Food Extraordinaire

Sea urchins (Axinioi) could hardly be imagined food for the gods, but the people of Paxos think so and most other Greek fishermen. A mysterious ritual takes place every month when the moon is full. The fishermen go out to gather great baskets of sea urchins but only the brown ones since the black ones have no eggs. Still alive and moving gently, the sea urchin is sliced in half, emptied of sea water and the top half retained. Inside the top half is a star shape of eggs, soft eggs which look like fish roe, and this is the prize. It takes an awful lot of sea urchins to collect a useful amount of eggs and this delicacy is eaten raw mixed with lemon and oil or it can be gently heated with yoghurt to make a cream sauce for use over spaghetti. Collecting the eggs is such a laborious business that it is usually only done for family consumption and it is unlikely to be found on a taverna menu.

the south which is appreciably nearer. The purpose of the visit to Antipaxos is mainly for its superb beaches and swimming. Since this is something that you can do without leaving Corfu, it might be considered that a longer visit to Paxos would be more interesting. If this is the case, search out a trip which only visits that island.

Antipaxos is a small island where grape vines or olive trees vastly outnumber permanent residents. It is separated from the southern tip of Paxos by a mere two nautical miles and the island itself has an area of three square kilometres. Cliffs mark the west coast but they are lower on the east coast and it has a couple of beaches which must rate amongst the finest in the Mediterranean. Vrika is the first one reached and where the boats usually dock although some also visit Voutoumi. Vrika's alluring combination of white sand and turquoise blue waters may seem like heaven on earth but Voutoumi Bay further south is within walking distance and just as beautiful. Both beaches have tavernas for refreshments. Holiday accommodation exists on the island in the form of houses and villas but not rooms. Anyone totally smitten who would like to return for a holiday some day should enquire at the taverna.

From Antipaxos the boat steams back to Paxos to dock at the attractive port of **Gaios** which is also the island's capital. Although much bigger than Antipaxos, Paxos is still only around 10km (6 miles) long and

4km (2½ miles) wide which means it does not take too long to walk across the island. There is no need to walk since there is a bus service which connects Gaios to the other main towns, Longos and Lakka, which run roughly every two hours (except on Sunday).

Paxos is the smallest of the principal Ionian islands with a permanent population of around 125. Covered by a green mantle of olive broken only by limestone cliffs, it is not too dissimilar from Corfu but, somehow, Paxos has managed to keep itself aloof from mass tourism. Difficulty with water supplies could be a reason or the high land prices. Perhaps the residents have witnessed the changes on Corfu and decided to remain unchanged. Whatever, Paxos remains a sleepy island which feels good from the very first moment.

The capital is named after Gaios, disciple of St Paul, who converted the island to Christianity. It is a charming and relaxing place which is almost enclosed by the nearby island of Ag Nikolaos with its ruined Venetian fort and the smaller lighthouse islet of Panagia. Unfortunately, the well preserved Venetian fort is not open to the public. Fishing boats add their colour to the waterfront promenade little disturbed by passing traffic. One event guaranteed to stir the sleepy atmosphere is the arrival of a new catch when the tangy smell of salt and fish draws crowds from nowhere. Mellow coloured nineteenth-century houses and shops line the harbour and threaded between are narrow streets which invite exploration. Here is where interesting little shops and tavernas are to be found although the main hub of life is the square which opens directly onto the harbour front. The tall, slightly dilapidated building to the north of the port which catches the eye is the old British residency of the High Commissioner. Sunbathers and swimmers will no doubt head for the small shingle beach just to the south of the town.

Whilst Gaios is the main town and busiest port, if there is time on the trip for an excursion, the choice will be between the second port Lakka, on the northern tip, and Longos (Loggos), also north but on the east coast. Distances are not too great and if the bus times are not convenient, try a taxi. **Lakka** faces into a shallow bay and has a fine shingle beach. There are tavernas but not too much to see except for its fine location, its aquarium and a Byzantine church. Small, intimate **Longos** is more picturesque and is regarded by many as the prettiest village on the island. The other option for an excursion is the round the island trips by boat to see the magnificent limestone cliffs and caves on the west coast. These leave Gaios usually around mid-morning.

Although Paxos is relatively small, it is criss-crossed with paths and tracks and offers good walking opportunities. Walking maps are available on the island.

FACTS FOR VISITORS

ACCOMMODATION

Hotels

These are classified by the GNTO (Greek National Tourist Office) into De Luxe, AA and A class which are subject to a minimum price structure only. Bars, restaurants and swimming pools are the facilities that you expect to find but, on a cautionary note, the class in itself is not a guarantee of the standard of service. All the luxury hotels on the island are to be found in or near Corfu town although usually there is at least one A category hotel to be found in most of the major resorts.

In addition there are B, C and D classes for which maximum and minimum room rates are fixed by the GNTO. These hotels are obliged to display their category and price behind the door of each room. There is no C in the Greek alphabet so this class is represented by the gamma sign G (g). Extra charges described as taxes or service may be added to the final rate and you need to check each time. Note that the charge is normally a room charge, not a charge per person and may or may not include breakfast. Room charges are seasonal with low, mid and high season rates. It is possible to bargain, especially for a stay of three days or more, but you are most likely to succeed when business is slack out of high season. Generally the C class hotels have rooms with bathrooms as do many of the D class but here it is not obligatory. Many of these hotels are often family run and offer a good level of cleanliness and comfort. The lower grade hotels may not have bar or restaurant facilities, except for breakfast.

Pensions

Accommodation of this kind in small hotels or private houses can also be very good. Again, the standards are controlled and graded by the GNTO but you really need to take each one on its own merit and do not hesitate to inspect before you commit yourself. At best they are very good with private bathroom facilities and a kindly Greek family to fuss over and take care of you. At worst you keep looking around!

Villas and Apartments

The vast bulk of the accommodation on Corfu falls into this category. Many, but not all, are in the hands of letting agencies who place them with tour operators. In early season a lot of apartments stand empty and,

Facing page: Danilia village

and even though they may be contracted out, it is still possible to make private arrangements on the spot, sometimes at very attractive rates. Otherwise, it is a question of driving around looking for Rooms to Let signs and making enquiries either locally or through the GNTO or the Tourist Police.

There are some 150 hotels on the island and a full list can be obtained from the Association of Corfu Hotels, 12 Stefanou Padova Street, 49100 Corfu, Greece, ☎ 0661 22635.

A short selection of the categories in various locations follows:

Corfu Town Area

(Telephone code 0661)

Corfu Hilton International (De-Luxe), Kanoni, 274 rooms, ☎ 36540-9; Fax 36551

Corfu Palace (De-Luxe), 106 rooms, ☎ 39485-7; Fax 31749

Bella Venizia (A), 32 rooms, ☎ 442290

Cavalieri Hotel (A), 50 rooms, ☎ 390041, Fax 39283

Arion Hotel (B), 105 rooms, ☎ 37950

Corfu Acrodilon Apartments (B) ☎ 61362

King Alkinoos Hotel (B) ☎ 39300-2 Fax 31898

Marina Beach Hotel, Anemomylos, (B), 102 rooms, ☎ 32783 Fax 46655

Archondiko Hotel (C) 29 rooms, ☎ 36950

Arkadion Hotel (C), 47 beds, ☎ 37671-2

Atlantis Hotel (C), 58 rooms, ☎ 35560-2, Fax 46480

Ag Gordis

(Telephone code 0661)

Ag Gordis Hotel (A) 209 rooms, ☎ 53320, Fax 52234

Acharavi

(Telephone code 0663)

Filorian Apartments (A) 20 apartments, ☎ 63107, Fax 34740

St Georges Bay Country Club (A) 60 apartments, ☎ 63225

Acharavi Beach Hotel (B) 43 rooms, ☎ 63102, Fax 63461

Alikes

(Telephone code 0661)

Kerkyra Golf Hotel (A) 240 rooms, ☎ 31785-7, Fax 38120

Alikes Beach (C) 24 rooms, ☎ 37628

Barbati

(Telephone code 0663)

Alexiou Hotel (B) 52 rooms, ☎ 91383, Fax 91087

Barbati Hotel (C) 15 rooms, ☎ 31570

Benitses

(Telephone code 0661)

San Stefano Hotel (A) 260 rooms, ☎ 36036, Fax 72272

Achilles Hotel (B) 74 rooms, ☎ 72425-6, Fax 72436

Belvedere Hotel (B) 180 rooms, ☎ 72442

Potomaki (B) 150 rooms, ☎ 30889, Fax 72451

Benitses Hotel (C) 16 rooms, ☎ 72248

La Miraz 21 rooms, ☎ 72026

Dassia

(Telephone code 0061)

Corfu Chandris (A), 301 rooms, ☎ 33871, Fax 93458

Elea Beach Hotel (A), 198 rooms, ☎ 93490-3, Fax 93494

Magna Grecia Hotel (A), 116 rooms, ☎ 93563, Fax 93396

Akti Palma Hotel (B), 37 rooms, ☎ 93941

Ekaterini Apartments (B), 18 apartments, ☎ 93350

Mystral Hotel (B), 25 rooms, ☎ 93511

Akti (C), 54 rooms, ☎ 93224, Fax 93224

Doria (C), 21 rooms, ☎ 93865 Oskar Hotel (C), 28 rooms, ☎ 93371, Fax 93971

Primavera Hotel (C), 50 rooms, ☎ 91911, Fax 91914

Glifada

(Telephone code 0661)

Grand Hotel (A) 242 rooms, ☎ 94201, Fax 37919

Glifada Akti Hotel (B) 35 rooms, ☎ 94254

Gouvia

(Telephone code 0661)

Corcyra Beach Hotel (A) 236 rooms, ☎ 30770-2, Fax 91591

Debono Hotel (A), 50 rooms, ☎ 91755-6, Fax 90009

Spiti Priftis Apartments (A), 23 rooms, ☎ 91585

Aspa Apartments (B), 18 rooms, ☎ 91165

Elisabeth Hotel (C), 22 rooms, ☎ 91451

Ipsos

(Telephone code 0661)

Ipsos Beach Hotel (B), 60 rooms, ☎ 93232

Mega Hotel (C) 32 rooms, ☎ 93208, Fax 93566

Kassiopi

(Telephone code 0663)

Poseidon Apartments (A) 6 apartments, ☎ 81439

Kavos

(Telephone code 0662)

San Marina Hotel (B) 56 rooms, ☎ 61345, Fax 22173

Alexander Beach (C) 28 rooms, ☎ 22281, Fax 23734

Liapades

(Telephone code 0663)

Elly Beach Hotel (A) 48 rooms, ☎ 41455, Fax 41479

Mora'i'tikia

(Telephone code 0661)

Miremare Beach (De-Luxe) 150 rooms, ☎ 30226-8, Fax 75305

Delfinia Hotel (A) 83 rooms, ☎ 30318

Bella Grecia (C) 37 rooms, ☎ 75056, Fax 75471

Nissaki

(Telephone code 0663)

Nissaki Beach (A) 239 rooms, ☎ 91232, Fax 22079

Paleokastritsa

(Telephone code 0663)

Akrotiri Beach (A) 126 rooms, ☎ 41275, Fax 41277

Oceanis Hotel (B) 72 rooms, ☎ 41229, Fax 22368

Paleokastritsa Hotel (B) 163 rooms, ☎ 22117, Fax 52234

Odysseus (C) 36 rooms, ☎ 41209, Fax 41342

Roda

(Telephone code 0663)

Coral Hotel (B) 30 rooms, ☎ 63490, Fax 63491

Roda Beach Hotel (B) 360 rooms, ☎ 63224, Fax 63436

Afroditi Hotel (C) 21 rooms, ☎ 63125

Silver Beach Hotel (C) 33 rooms, ☎ 63112, Fax 63076

Sidari

(Telephone code 0663)

Mimosa Hotel (C) 35 rooms, ☎ 95363, Fax 95361

Facing page: A wayside shrine

Three Brothers Hotel (C) 35 rooms, ☎ 95342, Fax 95343

Sinarades

(Telephone code 0661)

Yaliskari Palace (A) 245 rooms, ☎ 31400, Fax 52234

Camping

Camping in areas other than on official camping grounds is not permitted in any part of the island. It is something which the Greek authorities tend to get uptight about, especially in popular tourist regions. Finding a camp site on Corfu should not be a problem as there are some 15 sites scattered around the island. Further details from the Association of Greek Camping, 102 Solonos Street, 10680 Athens, ☎ 362 1560.

CAR HIRE

Car hire is popular and many visitors take a car for three or four days which is generally enough to see the various parts of the islands. A current driving licence is required for EU nationals and others should have an International Driving Permit. The hirer must be over 21 for a car and 25 for a jeep or a minibus. If there is any intention to take the car on ferries, it is not a problem but it must be sanctioned by the hire company.

Corfu is expensive for car hire and a better deal can be arranged by booking and paying in advance of departure, not necessarily through a tour company but through companies like Holiday Autos and Transhire ☎ 071 978 1922 and Fax 071 978 1797) which offer good rates and include full insurance and unlimited mileage. These companies operate through an agent on the island and offer rates significantly lower than those available from the agent on the spot.

There is no shortage of car hire companies on the island including internationally known agencies such as Avis, Hertz, Budget and Eurodollar. Advertised car hire rates are very often the basic rates exclusive of insurance, mileage and tax. Third party insurance is compulsory under Greek law and this cost will be added to the hire charge. An additional optional insurance is collision damage waiver (CDW) and it is imperative to take it. This cannot be stressed too strongly. Should you be unfortunate enough to be involved in an accident without CDW insurance and the costs cannot be recovered from a third party then the consequences can be frightening. At best you may be faced with a huge repair bill, at worst you could end up in jail until it is fully paid. On short one or two day hires mileage is limited to 100km (62 miles) a day and a rate applies for excess kilometres. On top of all this is VAT at 18 per cent.

Tyres and damage to the underside of the car are mostly excluded from the insurance cover. Take time when you are accepting the car to inspect the tyres and, if not fully satisfied, do not accept the vehicle. It is worth a moment too to check that lights and indicators are fully operational. Greek law demands that a car must also carry a fire extinguisher, first aid kit and a warning triangle.

Motorcycles

Above comments on insurance apply also to hiring a motor cycle or moped. There is a problem over crash helmets too. The law says very clearly that these must be worn but the chances that you will be able to hire them along with the bike are slim. Do ask since a number of agencies have helmets but only produce them if they think that they are about to lose some business. It is an unhappy situation which only compounds the personal dangers to motorcyclists in a country which has a very high accident rate. Make sure before you depart that the lights work. If you intend to hire a motorcycle, it is worth checking the fine print in the medical section of the holiday insurance taken out in your home country. Such is the concern over motorcycle accidents that some companies are specifically excluding injuries arising this way.

See also Driving on Corfu.

CHANGING MONEY

Banks are in extremely short supply outside Corfu town but there are plenty of Exchange Bureaux around to compensate. This is fine for visitors exchanging bank notes or Travellers Cheques but less convenient for holders of Eurocheques. For the latter the Bureaux charge a commission, usually 2 per cent, on top of the commission charged by the bank. Normally, the Bureaux are open for much longer hours than the bank, sometimes extending well into the evening. Hotels also offer exchange facilities but generally their rates are less favourable.

For those travelling into Corfu town to use the banks then the opening hours are as follows: Monday to Thursday 8am-2pm, Friday 8am-1.30pm. Automatic teller machines are at the moment only to be found in Corfu town and these generally accept Visa, Eurocheque and Master cards. Machines for exchanging notes too can be found in the town.

Post Offices sometimes offer exchange facilities and they are open on weekdays from 7.30am to 2pm. They are closed on Saturday and Sunday.

CONSULATES

Nearest foreign Embassies and Consulates are:

Australia
37 D Soutsou Street & An Tsocha 115 21 Athens
☎ 6447303

Canada
4 I. Genadou Street
115 21 Athens
☎ 7239511-9

Consular Help

Consular help is on hand in times of emergency but this is largely in an advisory capacity. The following comments are offered in terms of guide lines only and do not fully define the powers of the office. The Consul can:

Help with problems over a lost passport and issue an emergency one if necessary.

Help with problems over lost money or tickets but only by contacting relatives or friends at your request to ask them to provide the finance needed.

Advise on the details of transferring funds.

Encash a cheque supported by a valid banker's card but only in an emergency and as a last resort when there are no other options.

Make a loan to cover repatriation expenses when this is the absolute last resort.

Arrange for next of kin to be informed following an accident or death and advise on procedures.

Act for nationals arrested or imprisoned to inform relatives

Give guidance on organisations experienced in tracing missing people

Provide a list of local interpreters, English speaking doctors and solicitors .

They do not involve themselves in finding work or obtaining work permits. Neither will they investigate a crime, give legal advice, instigate legal procedures on your behalf or attempt to interfere with the Greek legal procedures. Nationals in hospital or imprisoned can only expect the same treatment as the Greeks and the Consul has no power to gain better conditions.

New Zealand
15 -17 Toscha Street
115 12 Athens
☎ 6410311-5

USA
Embassy-Consulate
91 Vass. Sophias Avenue
115 21 Athens
☎ 721951-9

UK
Consulate
1 Menekratous Street
Corfu Town
☎ 0661 30055 and 37995

CRIME AND THEFT

On an island like Corfu which receives many thousands of visitors annually, some crime and theft is inevitable but levels are low and incidence of violence is rare. There is no need to feel threatened in any way, even throughout the evening, but it is sensible to be cautious late at night, especially women on their own.

Many hotels have safety deposit boxes available for guests at a small charge. Otherwise, keep valuables out of sight. This is particularly true if you have a car. Cameras, personal stereos and the like are best carried with you but if you need to leave them in the car make sure they are locked in the boot.

If you are unfortunate enough to suffer a loss through theft or carelessness then report it to the Tourist Police. There is a form to complete if an insurance claim is contemplated.

If your loss includes a passport then you will need to contact your Consul. See page 113.

CURRENCY AND CREDIT CARDS

The local currency is the drachma which is indicated by drx or simply Dx (DR) before the number. Drachma notes commonly in circulation include 10,000, 5,000, 1,000 and 500 with just a few 100 and 50 drachma notes still around and coins of 100, 50, 20, 10 and 5 drachma value. The 100 and 50 drachma notes are steadily being replaced by coins but are still legal tender. The new 100, 50 and 20 drachma coins are all gold coloured and differ only in size. The 100 and 50 drachma coins in particular are easy to confuse. Some of the 20 drachma coins are still silver as are those of lesser value. Avoid bringing home coins and low value notes since most banks refuse to change them.

Travellers cheques, Eurocheques and hard currencies are freely accepted at banks, Post Offices and Exchange Bureaux. Credit cards and charge cards are also widely accepted in hotels, shops and restaurants especially in Corfu Town. While most of the larger petrol stations in town will accept credit cards, do not count on plastic to pay for petrol in the countryside.

Although it is possible to get a

Preceding page: Relaxing at Nissaki

cash advance on a credit card, there still seems to be some suspicion of this transaction. Only certain banks will co-operate and the best ones to try are the National Bank of Greece and the Commercial Bank. There is a minimum size of transaction, around 15,000 drachmas.

Always take your passport when changing money. Even though the production of a passport may not be a necessary requirement, the Greeks rely on them as a means of identification. You may even be asked for it when purchasing an internal flight ticket. The cost of changing money in terms of commission does vary and it pays to check; normally the cheapest place is at a bank and the worst place is at the hotel reception.

DRIVING ON CORFU

Driving on Corfu is on the right hand side of the road and overtaking on the left. In the event of an accident where the driver was proven to be on the wrong side of the road, the insurance is invalidated. Unless there are signs indicating otherwise, the speed limits are as follows: built-up areas 50kph (31mph), outside built-up areas 80kph (50mph). Seat belts must be worn by law. The use of main beam headlights in towns and cities is forbidden as is the carrying of petrol in cans.

Unleaded petrol (*amolivthi venzini*) is freely available on Corfu but not always in the country areas. The grades of petrol (*venzini*) normally on offer are unleaded, Super-un-leaded and Super at 96/98 octane. Diesel is also widely available and, like petrol, is sold by the litre.

Parking in Corfu Town is not too much of a problem if the pay car park is used opposite the Old Fort. Street parking is a problem since there are plenty of parking restrictions, often ignored by the Greeks but illegal parking can result in a ticket and a hefty fine. The ticket indicates the amount of the fine and where and when to pay it. The police are not empowered to collect on the spot fines.

With one of the worst accident rates in Europe, driving in Greece demands a cautious attitude from the onset. The discipline shown by the majority of drivers in western European countries, which brings order to traffic flow, is often missing from Greek drivers but Corfiot drivers are a little more orderly. Drive with your own safety in mind. Another major hazard is the state of the roads. Pot holes are a serious danger and can be encountered unexpectedly even on well surfaced roads. Some of the holes are large enough to cause damage to tyres and wheels. A line of rocks on the road guiding you towards the centre is the usual warning of edge subsidence and there will often be no warning signs. Minor roads, which are well surfaced, may suddenly become unmetalled. Road works may have no hazard warning signs or irregular ones such as a pile of earth or a milk crate with a flag.

Here is a quick check on some of

Above: This island is passed as you approach the jetty north of Gaios

the hazards frequently encountered: uncertain rights of way, limited road markings, narrow roads, sharp edges, potholes, tight hairpins, ill placed road signs, Greek drivers driving the wrong way through a one way system, sheep, goats and donkeys, motorcyclists without lights, and pedestrians where there are no footpaths.

Information on all aspects of motoring can be obtained from the Automobile Association & Touring Club of Greece, ELPA, Athens Tower, 2-4, Messogion Street, 15 27 Athens, ☎ 7791 615 to 629 and 7797 402 to 405

Road Signs

Fortunately, international road signs are used throughout the island but there may be occasions when you encounter temporary signs written in Greek. Here are a few examples:

ΑΛΤ – Stop
ΕΛΑΤΤΩΣΑΤΕΤΑΧΥΤΗΑΝ — Reduce speed
ΕΡΓΑΕΠΙΤΗΣΟΔΟΥ — Road works in Progress
ΑΝΩΜΑΑΙΑΟΔΟΣΤΡΩΜΑΤΟΣ — Bad road surface
ΑΠΑΓΟΡΕΥΕΤΑΙΤΟΠΡΟΣΠΕΡΑΣΜΑ — No overtaking
ΤΕΛΟΣ ΑΠΗΓΟΡΕΥΜΕΝΗΣ ΖΩΝΗΣ — End of no-overtaking
ΠΑΡΑΚΑΜΠΤΗΡΙΟΣ —Diversion
ΜΟΝΟΔΡΟΜΟΣ — One-way traffic
ΠΟΡΕΙΑ ΥΠΟΧΡΕΩΤΙΚΗ ΔΕΞΙΑ — Keep right
ΑΠΑΓΟΡΕΥΕΤΑΙΗΣΤΑΘΜΕΥΣΙΣ — No parking

Above: The harbour area at Gaios on Paxos

Below: If you are relying on buses, Paleokastritsa is worth visiting

ΑΔΙΕΞΟΔΟΣ — No through road

Accidents and Legal Advice

In the event of an accident involving personal injury or damage to property, both the law and your insurance require that it is reported to the police. Start by contacting the tourist police by dialling (0661) 39503 or outside Corfu town the Rural Police on 109 and ask their advice.

ELPA offer free legal advice concerning Greek legislation on car accidents and insurance.

Breakdowns

It is a legal requirement to place a warning triangle 100m (109yd) behind the car. Next step is to contact the car hire agency or if the car is private, contact Elpa by dialling 104. Elpa has reciprocal arrangements with European motoring organisations, like the British AA.

DISABLED FACILITIES

Whilst there is an awareness of this problem, few practical steps have been taken to improve matters. As yet only the international hotels provide anything like adequate facilities. Outside Corfu town, very few places have pavements and where present they are often full of trees making passage difficult in places. Ramps up and down pavements are few and far between.

ELECTRICITY

Mains electricity is supplied at 220 volts AC. Electrical equipment should be fitted with a continental two pin plug or an appropriate adapter used. A wide selection of adapters for local plugs to interchange between two and three pin (not UK three pin) are available cheaply on the island.

EMERGENCY TELEPHONE NUMBERS

Ambulance: 166
Emergency Road
   Assistance (ELPA): 104
Fire: 199
First Aid: 0661 30562
Lost property: 0661 39294
Municipal Police: 100
Rural Police: 109
Tourist Police: 0661 39503

GREEK TIME

Greek normal time is 2 hours ahead of GMT. The clocks advance one hour for summertime starting the last Sunday in March and ending the last Sunday in September.

America and Canada: Greek normal time is ahead of time in America, 7 hours ahead of Eastern Standard, 8 hours ahead of Central, 9 hours ahead of mountain and 10 hours ahead of Pacific Time

Australia and New Zealand; Greek normal time is 7BD hours behind South Australia, 8 hours behind New South Wales, Tasmania and Victoria and 10 hours behind time in New Zealand. These differences relate to GMT but, to take into account clock changes for Daylight Saving hours, the following corrections should be made: add 1 hour to these differences from late September to the end of March and subtract 1 hour from late March to the end of September.

HEALTH CARE

For minor ailments like headaches, mosquito bites or tummy upsets, head for the chemist shop (*farmakion*). If you need a further supply of prescription drugs make sure to take a copy of your prescription and the chances are that you will be able to get them, and cheaply too. Pharmacies are open normal shop hours and most seem to speak English. Certain chemist shops are on rota to provide a 24 hour service and information for the nearest is posted in the pharmacy window.

If it is a doctor or dentist you require, the chemist shop should again be able to assist. If that does not work then contact the Tourist Police. There are plenty of English speaking doctors and dentists on Corfu.

Problems really start if hospital treatment is required. European countries have reciprocal arrangements with the Greeks for free medical treatment, subject to certain restrictions. For this reason British visitors should take an E111 form obtained from the Post Office. The story does not end there. To operate the scheme you need to find the local Greek Social Insurance office (IKA) who, after inspecting your E111, will direct you to a registered doctor or dentist. If you are in a region remote from the IKA office which is in Corfu Town then you must pay privately for your treatment and present your bills to an IKA official before you leave Corfu. Up to half your costs may be refunded. The best answer is to ensure that you have adequate holiday insurance cover.

Emergency treatment for sunburn, broken bones etc, is free in state hospitals. The situation is less happy if you require treatment as an in-patient. In many of these hospitals, nursing care is restricted only to medical treat-ment and it is left to the family to supply general nursing care, drinks, food and even blankets.

It is generally preferable to activate private medical insurance.

HEALTH HAZARDS

Stomach upsets are perhaps the most common ailment. The excessive olive oil used in cooking and over salads can be a cause of queezy stomachs so take care with oily foods, at least to start with. The digestive system adjusts to this within a few days and you can soon eat giant beans swimming in oil without fear. Squeeze plenty of fresh lemon over your food to counter the oil and, if still troubled, an acidic drink, like Coca-Cola, helps to settle things. Drinking wine to excess can cause similar symptoms too. More serious are the upsets caused by bad water and bad food. Generally on Corfu it is better to drink bottled water which is freely available and cheap in the shops and supermar-

kets. Avoiding food poisoning is not always possible but there are elementary precautions that can help. Many tavernas prepare cooked dishes for the lunch time trade and these are left keeping warm until finally sold. If they are still there in the evening, and they often are, avoid them. Ask for something which will require grilling or roasting.

See also Mosquitoes page 126.

HOLIDAY INSURANCE

Whichever holiday insurance you choose, make sure that the cover for medical expenses is more than adequate. It helps too if there is an emergency 24 hour contact to take care of arrangements, including repatriation if necessary. Injuries caused whilst taking part in certain hazardous pursuits are normally excluded from medical cover. Look carefully at the specified hazardous pursuits; in recent times, injuries caused by riding a moped or motorbike have been added to the list by some insurers.

INTERNATIONAL DIALLING CODES

Codes from Greece are as follows: UK and Northern Ireland 0044: United States and Canada 001: Australia 0061: New Zealand 0064.

See also Telephone Services.

LANGUAGE

Many Greeks speak good English and they certainly do on Corfu. Children learn it in state schools and most of them attend private schools as well. After all, English is the official second language in Greece and all official notices are presented in Greek and English, at least the more recent notices. Therein lies the danger. It is all too easy to expect and rely on every Greek to speak English which is clearly not the case when you move into country areas.

Some knowledge of the Greek language is not only useful to help you get by, but can enhance enormously the pleasure of your holiday. The Corfiots really warm to you if you make the slightest effort with their language. Do not worry about perfection in pronunciation in the beginning, just give it a go. The Greeks are very outgoing and, if they have any English, they will try it out no matter how fractured it is. Take a leaf from their book. As long as you make an effort, the Greeks will love you for it and once you can string a few words together you might find their hospitality overwhelming.

Perhaps the biggest hurdle to getting started is the Greek alphabet itself. If you take a little time to study it, you will find it is not really so different. Isolate the letters which are unique to the Greek alphabet and the remainder generally follow the sequence of the English alphabet. The language is phonetic so time taken over learning the sounds of the letters will be well rewarded in subsequent progress. Two pieces of

Facing page: The bell tower of Viacherna Convent

advice to get you started on the right foot. (1) Treat all vowels equally and do not attempt to lengthen them. (2) Avoid breaking a word down into syllables as in English, instead, follow the stress pattern indicated by the accent in the word.

The Alphabet

Dipthongs
ai **e** in met
an **av** as in avoid or **af** in after
eu **ev** as in ever or **ef** as in left
oi **e** as in feet
ou **oo** as in mood

Double consonants
mp — b at the beginning of words; mb in the middle
vt — d at the beginning of words; nd in the middle
tz — dz as in adze
gg = ng — in the middle of a word
gk = g — g at the beginning; ng in the middle

Numbers

The numbers 1, 3 and 4 (and all numbers ending in them) have three forms, masculine, feminine and neteur. In this list the phonetic words are given in place of the Greek.
1 — ena (n), enas (m) or mia (f)
2 — theo
3 — tria (n), tris (m & f)
4 — tessera (n), tessaris (m & f)
5 — pende
6 — eksi
7 — efta
8 — octo
9 — enya
10 — theka
11 — entheka
12 — thotheka
13 — theka tria
14 — theka tessera
        etc up to twenty
20 — eekosee
21 — eekosee ena (n & m), mia (f)
30 — treeanda
40 — seranda
50 — peninda
60 — eksinda
70 — evthominda
80 — ogthonda
90 — eneninda
100 — ekato
130 — ekato treeanda
200 — thea-kosea
300 — tria-kosea
1000 — hilia

Days of the week:

Monday — Theftera
Tuesday — Treetee
Wednesday — Tetartee
Thursday — Pemptee
Friday — Paraskevee
Saturday — Savato
Sunday — Kiriakee

Months of the year:

January — Eeanuareos
February — Fevruareos
March — Marteos
April — Apreeleos
May — Maeos
June — Eeuneos
July — Eeuleos
August — Avyustos
September — Septemvreos
October — Octovreos
November — Noemvreos
December — Thekemvreos

Useful phrases:

Yes — neh
No — ockee
Please — parakalo
Thank you — efharreesto
Hello and goodbye — yasas
Good morning — kaleemera
Good evening — kaleespera
Goodnight — kaleeneekta
How are you? — tee kanete?
Do you speak English? —
        meelatee angleeka
When? — poteh?
I want — thelo

Where is/are? — poo eene?
... the post office? — poo eene to takeethromeeo?
... the tourist office — poo eene to grafeeo toureesmoo?
... the museum? — poo eene to mooseeo?
... the bus station — poo eene o stathmos ton leoforeeon?
... the toilets — poo eene ee tooaletes?

Hotel — ksenothoheeo
Perhaps you have.. — meepos ekehteh
.. a single room — ena mono thomateeo
...a double room — ena theeplo thomateeo
...with bath — meh banyeeo
...with shower — meh dush

Shop — to magazee
Market — agora
How much? — posso?
How many? — possa?
How much does it cost? — posso kanee?
How much do they cost? — posso kanoonee?
Open/closed — anikto/kleesto
Stamp(s) — gramatossimo/ gramatossima
Envelope(s) — fakelo(a)
One kilo — ena kilo
Half a kilo — meeso kilo
Two kilo — heo kila
Apple(s) — meelo(a)
Orange(s) — portokalee(eea)
Tomatoes — domates
Cucumber — angouree
Lettuce — maroolee

Doctor — yatros
Pharmacy — farmakeeo
Hospital — nosokomeeo
Police — asteenomeea

Place Names

With no official transliteration, the latinisation of the Greek alphabet is open to various interpretations which leads to much confusion. The conversion of the double consonants, for example, is one cause of difficulty. The Greek **nt** is pronounced as **d** at the start of a word but **nd** in the middle. A Greek word starting with **nt** is almost invariably Latinised to begin with **d** but in the middle of the word both **nt** and **nd** can be observed. This is a problem on Corfu particularly since it is invariably Latinised to **nt**, as in Kontokali, but it is actually pronounced Kondokali. Similarly, Pantokrator should be Pandokrator. The same sort of situation arises with the Greek letters **mp** which transliterate to **b** at the beginning of the word but **mb** in the middle. Again on Corfu this is Latinised to **mp** which leads to the incorrect pronunciation. This is seen in Trumpeta when it should really be Trumbeta.

Vowel sounds, especially **e** and **i**, do not always strictly correspond so there is a tendency to substitute the more phonetically correct. Some single consonants have no strict equivalent either, such as **X**, pronounced as the **ch** in loch, and this is Latinised to **ch**, which is a mile away phonetically, or **h** which is a little better. The village of Xora appears as Chora or Hora. All these difficulties are reflected in the spelling of place names. Pick up three different maps and it is more than likely that many of the same villages will have three different spellings. The philosophy adopted for this book is firstly to follow the spelling observed on the sign outside the village or, since many villages are without name boards, use the spelling which leads to a more accurate pronunciation.

LEFT LUGGAGE

There are left luggage facilities in the area of the New Port, Corfu Town, look for signs.

LOST PROPERTY

This should be reported immediately to the Tourist Police, Spilia Square, Corfu Town, ☎ 39503. It is particu-

larly important if an insurance claim is to be made. For enquiries about items left in a taxi, ring 0661 38071.

MAPS

On the whole, maps of Corfu are more accurate than for many other Greek islands but still not wholly reliable. The main roads are accurately marked but the position of joining roads does not necessarily relate to reality nor does the indication of the surface. Generally, the signposting is fairly good on the island with the Greek signs displayed first and the Latinised version a little nearer the junction.

MOSQUITOES

Mosquitoes feed most actively at dusk and dawn but they can still be a nuisance throughout the evening and the night. If you sit or dine outside in the evening, particularly near trees, either cover up your arms and legs or use insect repellent. For the hotel room, an electric machine which slowly vaporises a pellet is very effective, especially with the windows closed and there are sprays available for more instant results if intruders are spotted. Anthisan cream is an effective calming treatment for bites, particularly if applied immediately.

MUSEUMS

There is a charge for admission except on a Sunday when entrance is free to all but private museums.

Above: The ruins at Kassope where Aphrodite was worshipped

Below: Parga beach

Monday is now the general closing day.

The museums are closed too, or open only for a short while, on certain public holidays which include 1 January, 25 March, Good Friday and Easter Monday, 1 May and 25 and 26 December. In addition they have half-days on Shrove Monday, Whitsunday, 15 August, 28 October and Epiphany, 6 January.

NATIONAL TOURIST OFFICE

The Greek National Tourist Office in Corfu Town is newly located on Rizospasto near the junction with Polila. The telephone numbers are unchanged and are 0661 37638-40 and 37520.

NEWSPAPERS AND MAGAZINES

The *Financial Times*, most British newspapers, a selection from European countries and the *Herald Tribune* are usually available in virtually all centres of tourism. Mostly they are one day late and sometimes more. Expect a fair mark up in price. The place to look for newspapers is in the tourist shops, supermarkets and at the kiosks (*periptera*) where you will see them on racks or along the counter.

Also available in Corfu town on the day of issue is *Athens News*, published in the English language. It contains a mix of local and international stories but the entertainment section announcing events and concerts relates only to Athens. The English language is constantly being pushed into areas where no man has dared before but, notwithstanding, it gives an interesting insight into Greek attitudes.

A selection of English and European magazines is also available.

NIGHTLIFE

Discos are to be found in most resorts around the island and displays of Greek dancing are laid on in many restaurants and tavernas. Some of the more famous hot spots include Danilia Village for a very traditional Greek night (☎ 0661 91621) with food, music and dancing, Corfu by Night which is a taverna/night club with cabaret and Greek dancing and the Tripa taverna where you can eat and drink as much as you like for a set price and be entertained by Greek dancers.

NUDISM

Topless bathing is commonplace on all public beaches on Corfu. Nude bathing is not acceptable on public beaches but is practised with discretion on some of the more remote and secluded beaches although these are increasingly difficult to find.

PETS

Cats and dogs require health and rabies inoculation certificates issued by a veterinary authority in the country of origin not more than 12 months (cats 6 months) and not less than 6 days prior to arrival.

PHARMACIES

Pharmacies open Monday and Wednesday 8am-2.30pm. Tuesday, Thursday, and Friday 8am-2pm and 5-8pm. There is also a duty rosta for Pharmacies so that at least one in the vicinity is open on Saturday and Sunday. Usually a note on the door of the pharmacy details the duty chemist.

PHOTOGRAPHY

Signs which show a picture of a camera crossed out indicate a prohibited area for photography. Notices of this kind are posted near every military establishment, no matter how small or insignificant. Disregard this at your peril. The Greeks are still paranoiac about security and anyone found using a camera in a prohibited zone faces unpleasant consequences. The photographer is normally held in custody whilst the film is developed and inspected. It could mean overnight detention.

Photography with a camera mounted on a tripod is prohibited in museums as is the use of flash in some. Video cameras are often subject to a fee.

Outdoors, the light for photography is brilliant. Summer haze can cause difficulties with distant shots but the use of a UV or Skylight filter is helpful here. Some of the clearest days occur in spring when a dry east wind blows. Midday light is harsh and contrasty, mornings and evening provide the best lighting conditions for serious photography.

POSTAL SERVICES

Post Offices open on weekdays from 7.30am-2pm. They are closed on Saturday and Sunday.

Stamps (*grammatosima*) can be purchased at the post office, sometimes at a special counter, or at a kiosk (*periptero*). They are also available in many shops and some of the larger hotels but at a slightly increased price.

Letters from Greece to overseas destinations are delivered fairly speedily, 4/6 days for Europe, 6/8 for America and longer for Australia and New Zealand. For a speedier delivery, ask for express post on which there is a fairly modest surcharge but it cuts 2/3 days off the delivery time.

A telegram, telex or fax can be sent from the telephone office, the OTE although some tour agency offices also provide a service.

PUBLIC HOLIDAYS AND FESTIVALS

The Greek calendar overflows with red letter days; public holidays, Saints days and festivals. On public holidays, banks, shops and offices are closed although restaurants and tavernas normally stay open. Public transport is often interrupted too, reverting either to a Sunday service or to none at all. Petrol stations also close for many of the holidays. The days to watch out for are:

Above: A festival in Corfu town

Below: A general view of the Parga coastline, towards the castle

1 January — New Year's Day

6 January — Epiphany

25 March — Greek Independence Day

Monday before Lent — Clean Monday

April — Good Friday and Easter Monday

1 May — May Day

21 May — Ionian Day, commemorating union with Greece

Whit Monday

15 August — Assumption of the Blessed Virgin Mary

28 October — 'Ochi' Day

25 December — Christmas Day

26 December — Boxing Day

Easter is variable and does not always coincide with Easter throughout the rest of Europe.

Name-days are one reason why the calendar is so full of celebrations. It has been a long tradition for Greeks to ignore birthdays to celebrate instead the special day of their saint, and there are a lot of saints. If you see people wandering around with cake boxes neatly tied with fancy ribbon, or bunches of flowers or unusual activity around one of the many churches, then the chances are that it is a name day. The custom is for the person celebrating to offer hospitality to friends, to neighbours and to almost anyone who will partake of a little ouzo and refreshments.

Some of the big name days to watch out for are:

23 April — St George's day; all Georges everywhere celebrate their special day but in addition it is also the national day of Greece.

21 May — Saints Konstantinos and Eleni.

29 June — St Peter and St Paul

15 August — Assumption of the Blessed Virgin Mary. This is the day when millions of Marias celebrate and an important day in the religious calendar often marked by local pilgrimages or festivals.

8 November — for all Michaels and Gabriels.

6 December — the feast of St. Nicholas.

12 December — St Spiridon's day, the island's own saint.

Easter, the biggest and the most important celebration of the year, is especially important on Corfu and Easter weekend attracts visitors to the island from all over Greece. The arrival of Carnival time starts the long build up. This festival takes place throughout the three weeks before Lent and may commence as early as late January. Fancy dress is an important part of the tradition throughout the whole of Greece. It arises from the period of Turkish occupation when the Greeks were banned from conducting these celebrations. Driven under cover, festivities continued with people disguised to prevent recognition. Now it is firmly rooted into the custom and fancy dress and costumes are worn at all events. The children wander the streets in fancy dress and traditionally show defiance by wearing their disguises on the last school day of Carnival.

All this comes to an abrupt end with a complete change of mood on 'Clean Monday' (Kathari Deutera), the Monday before Lent. This is a public holiday when families traditionally exodus to the country to fly kites and to picnic, which mostly means heading to a taverna. Special meat-free menus are the order of the day.

It is back to the quiet life throughout Lent which is still strictly observed by many, especially in country regions. Serious preparations for Easter start on Maundy Thursday. How hens are persuaded to lay so actively for the occasion remains a mystery but shoppers are out buying eggs, not by the tens but by the hundreds. The rest of the day is spent in boiling the eggs and dying them red in the process. The colour red is supposed to have protective powers and the first egg dyed belongs to the Virgin.

Good Friday is a day of complete fast and widely observed. In tourist regions tavernas are open and life goes on as normal but in country areas it can be difficult or impossible to find food. Yellow or brown 'impure' candles are on sale everywhere ready for the evening church service. The sombre mood of the day is heightened by the continual tolling of church bells. It is a day for remembering their own dead; graves are visited and wreaths are laid. In the evening, the burial of Christ is the most moving and widely attended service in the whole of the Greek Orthodox calendar. The Epitaphios, the funeral bier of Christ, is centre stage in the services which start around 9 o'clock in the evening. Garlanded with fresh flowers and with a gilded canopy, the Epitaphios bearing the coffin of Christ is ceremoniously taken from church in dignified candle-lit procession followed by silent mourners and accompanied by bands playing solemn music. The processions from all the local churches meet in the town square for a further short service. This is the most poignant moment of the evening, cafés close, tavernas close and there is not one Greek who would willingly miss it. The processions return slowly to their churches, stopping at each street corner for a short prayer.

Saturday brings an air of expectancy and there is an unusual event here on the island not normally part of Easter celebrations elsewhere. Just before noon the streets are cleared and pots are thrown from the balconies into the street. The origins of this custom are uncertain but it is thought to represent the stoning of Judas. For the evening service, yellow candles are replaced with white. Funereal drapes are removed in the churches and decorations of laurel and myrtle take their place. In dimly lit churches everywhere, services begin. Slowly the light intensity increases reaching full brightness at midnight when priests triumphantly chant 'Christ is risen' (*Christos anesti*). The sanctuary doors open to show that the Epitaphios is empty. Light from the priest's candle is passed to the congregation and that flame is rapidly passed from candle to candle until it reaches the waiting crowds outside. Fire crackers drown the clamour of the church bells as the crowd erupts in joyous celebration and greetings of *'Christos anesti'* ring out loudest of all. The crowds disperse shortly, carefully protecting their burning candle; it is a good omen to enter the home with the flame still burning and make a sooty sign of the cross on the door lintel.

Sunday is a day of out-and-out rejoicing. The big occasion of the day is roasting the lamb or goat. Charcoal fires are lit early in the morning and the spit roasting is done with loving care over some 5 hours with copious quantities of ouzo or retsina to help things along. All those red eggs now appear and are used in friendly competition. Each contestant taps their egg hard enough to break an opponents but not their own.

Easter Monday has no special ceremonies or rituals and passes as any normal public holiday.

Cultural Events

Religious fairs, (*panayiria*), are commonplace in the summer months. *Panayiria* are a celebra-

tion of the name day of a particular church or monastery and usually held in the vicinity of the establishment. Celebrations are colourful, often beginning on the eve of the name day and continue throughout the actual day. Eating, drinking and dancing are central to any celebration for the Greeks so the barbecue is certain to be in operation. When the crowds are big enough, the vendors join in selling just about anything, baubles, bangles and beads.

St Spiridon, the island's patron saint, is central to celebrations on four occasions throughout the year. See A Day Out in Corfu Town, page 45 for further details.

A word of warning too. Each town and village has its own saint's day and sometimes, depending on the local whim and the phase of the moon, a holiday is called. This decision is often not taken until the day before so there is no way you can plan for such eventualities.

PUBLIC TOILETS

The most usual sign is WC with figures to indicate ladies (*gynaikon*) and gents (*andron*). Toilets in Corfu Town, in the Esplanade, are surprisingly good and above the standard normally found in Greece. There are also toilets in museums and at archaeological sites which are also good. Toilet paper is sometimes supplied where there is an attendant and very occasionally elsewhere. Take your own supply.

Clothes Sizes

Mens Suits:

UK/US		36	38	40	42	44	46
48							
Greece	46	48	50	52	54	56	58

Dress Sizes:

UK	8	10	12	14	16	18
US	6	8	10	12	14	16
Greece	34	36	38	40	42	44

Facing page: Ermones beach with its funicular

Below: A beach scene at Glifada

PUBLIC TRANSPORT

Buses

The bus service on Corfu is good and it offers a reliable way to see the island. The biggest problem is buses on popular routes get overcrowded in season and it may be difficult to board one at an intermediate stop.

There are two types of bus services on the island, the blue buses which serve Corfu town and local destinations, like Kanoni, and long distance green buses which serve outlying towns on the island. The bus station for the green buses, and for the Athens and Thessaloniki buses, lies on Avramiou street which runs between the New Port and San Rocco Square. Local buses start from San Rocco Square except for the Kanoni and Vassili buses which start from the Esplanade Square.

Printed timetables are usually available from the Tourist Office. The frequency of services is much less in winter but builds up as the tourist season gets underway. Throughout May the timetable changes weekly until the service reaches its maximum frequency sometime in June which is then held until early September. The timetable holds equally from Monday through to Saturday but Sunday sees a reduction in the number of buses to about half.

Taxis

Radio taxis can be called by telephoning 0661 33811-2 or 41333 from anywhere on the island. There are a number of taxi ranks in Corfu town including San Rocco Square, Spianada Square and Spilia Square by the New Port. Taxis are available in most of the tourist resorts.

Greek taxi drivers are not the most honest in the world and it pays either to check the price before the journey, if it is for a lengthy ride, or better still, insist that the meter be used. This displays the cumulative fare in drachmas. The rate of charges and surcharges are all fixed. Within the city boundaries taxi fares are charged at the single rate and you may see '1' displayed in a solitary box on the meter. Once you travel outside the city boundary, the double rate applies so it is likely you will see the driver alter the meter so that '2' shows in the box. Legitimate small surcharges are allowed for a sizeable piece of luggage, for attending an airport or port for the benefit of passengers, and for late night or very early morning travel. Surcharges are permitted too at holiday times, especially Christmas and Easter. Picking up a second fare is allowed too so you may find yourself sharing a taxi.

RADIO

The ERT1 radio station on Corfu (1008kHz or 91.8mHz) gives a daily weather forecast in English at 6.30am and news bulletins in English, French and German at 7.40am. ERT2 (981kHz) has news bulletins in English and French twice a day at 2.20pm and 9.20pm .

SHOPPING

Regulations on opening hours have changed recently to adjust to market needs. Different regions have their own views on this so there is now greater confusion than ever over opening times. Big supermarkets and department stores open: Monday to Friday 8am-8pm. Saturday 8am-3pm. Other shops open Monday and Wednesday 8am-2.30pm. Tuesday, Thursday, and Friday. 8am-2pm and 5pm-8pm.

In tourist areas, shopping hours are much more relaxed. Tourist shops and supermarkets in particular are open all day long but butchers, bakers and the like tend to observe more restricted hours.

SPORTS AND PASTIMES

Windsurfing:
Many of the small bays and coves are ideally suited to this sport and boards can be hired in most holiday resorts. Favoured spots for the experts are the west coast which enjoys a prevailing northwest wind in summer. Lessons for beginners are generally available too at rates which are still very reasonable.

Water-skiing and Jet skiing:
Available at many of the larger resorts as well as parascending.

Scuba diving:
Strictly prohibited unless in the control of a recognised diving school and only in designated areas. With so many antiquities in the waters around Greece, it is forbidden to remove anything from the sea bed and infringements normally result in a prison sentence. Diving schools operate in Paleokastritsa (Barracuda Club) Ipsos (Waterhoppers Diving Centre) with smaller clubs at Ag Gordis and Ermones Beach.

Tennis:
Courts are mostly to be found in the better class hotels but some allow non residents to use the facilities for a charge. Corfu Town has a tennis club at 4 Romanou Street near the Archaeological Museum and its four asphalt courts are available to non-members between 8am and 12noon.

Golf:
The island's only golf course in Ropa Valley, Corfu Golf Club, is highly respected and welcomes visitors. Telephone 0661 94220 for enquiries and T reservations. Buggies and trolleys are also available for hire. Competitions are held in May and October.

Horse-riding:
The island's countryside has a network of bridleways offering very attractive rides. Riding stables are scattered around the island at Gouvia (0661 30770), Alikes, Potamou (0661 31785) and the Ropa Valley Riding Sta-

bles (0661 94220). There are other stables so enquire locally.

Walking:

Corfu provides abundant opportunities for walking in the countryside and walking guides are available.

Sailing:

This is extremely popular around the coast of Corfu and most resorts have boats for hire. There is a 350 berth marina for yachts at Gouvia with support facilities with further berths available in Corfu Town, particularly just south of the Old Fort.

Yachts are freely available for hire either with or without crews if the charterer can prove competence with a recognised proficiency certificate.

SUNBATHING

Sunburn and sunstroke can easily spoil your holiday and considerable care needs to be exercised, especially in the early days. The sun is very burning even on a hazy day so great care is needed in protecting yourself and high factor sun creams should be used. Crawling beneath a parasol is not necessarily the full answer since the sun's rays reflect to some extent from the sand. Avoid, if possible, sunbathing in the middle of the day, from 10am until around 2.00pm when the sun it at its highest and most

direct. Sun creams help considerably but, at least for the first few days, take some very light clothing to cover up and control the exposure of your skin to the sun. A slowly acquired tan lasts longer.

Even mild sunburn can be painful and may cause a chill feeling but if fever, vomiting or blistering occurs then professional help is essential.

TELEPHONE SERVICES

Hotels usually offer a telephone service, often from the room, but expect to pay a premium for the convenience.

Telephone booths on the island have now been modernised to take phone cards and these are both convenient and economical. Cards, loaded with 100 units, are available often from the shop or periptero nearest the booth and the cost per unit is exactly the same as the OTE (Telecommunications office) charge. There is an OTE office in Corfu Town and mobile ones operating from vans in some of the bigger resorts. Here metered phones are available with a pay at the desk system. The advantage of the OTE is that payment is made only for the units used whereas a card may be more units than required.

In the main holiday resorts a number of tourist agencies offer a telephone service and often call themselves telephone exchanges.

Facing Page: The long sandy beach at Kavos

Although sometimes convenient, they are run for profit so expect to pay a higher rate.

International dialling codes from Greece are as follows: UK and Northern Ireland 0044: United States and Canada 001: Australia 0061: New Zealand 0064.

TIPPING

There are no hard and fast rules on tipping, especially since bills by law already include a 17 per cent service charge. Normally, the Greeks simply leave behind the small change after a meal and perhaps the best guide is to reward only for good service in a restaurant. Taxi drivers expect a tip as does the chamber maid in the hotel otherwise it is entirely by discretion.

WATER

Sources of drinking water vary on the island and all should be regarded as not suitable to drink unless otherwise advised. Bottled water is freely available.

INDEX

Published by:
Moorland Publishing Co Ltd,
Moor Farm Road West, Ashbourne,
Derbyshire DE6 1HD England

ISBN 0 86190 597 0

British Library Cataloguing in Publication Data:
a catalogue record for this book is available from the British Library.

Colour origination by: g.a. Graphics

Printed in Hong Kong by Wing King Tong

DEDICATION:
To son Neil, Christine and Hayley

PICTURE CREDITS:
All pictures are by the authors except pages: 7, 10 (top), 15 (top), 19 (top),
27 (bottom), 31 (bottom), 38, 42/43, 54, 55, 58 (both), 63 (both), 71 (bottom),
74 (bottom), 75, 83, 86, 90 (both), 91 (both), 94 (bottom), 95, 98 (top), 99, 102 (top),
107, 119 (both), 135, which are from the MPC Picture Collection,
and page 98 (bottom) which is by B Haines.

MPC Production Team:
Editor: Christine Haines
Designer: Dick Richardson
Cartographer: Mark Titterton

DISCLAIMER

While every care has been taken to ensure that the information in this
book is as accurate as possible at the time of publication, the publishers
and author accept no responsibility for any loss, injury or inconvenience
sustained by anyone using this book.

Your trip to Corfu should be a happy one, but certain activities such
as water sports should be approached with care and under proper
supervision when appropriate. It is also in your own interests to check
locally about flora and fauna that it is best to avoid.